Foundation for Search Operations

Searching for a Missing Person in a Non-Wilderness Area

Written and Edited

By

Coleman P. Brown III

Michael J. Zabetakis

Published by

AceVector Consulting, LLC
Hampstead, MD

Copyright © 2019

1st Printing Version 1.0
2nd Printing Version 2.0 (2020)
3rd Printing Version 3.0 (2022)

Disclaimer: This text is not an inclusive guide to search and rescue nor the complete instruction manual for search and rescue skills, management, or technical response to various search operations. The materials are not meant to replace practical training by competent search, rescue, and/or emergency response and instructional leaders or to replace actual experience.

The authors of this textbook are advocates for investigation by law enforcement. It is the duty of every law enforcement agency, volunteer group, or AHJ – Authority Having Jurisdiction or government agency with the responsibility in searching for lost or missing persons to obtain the knowledge, skill, and abilities as well as proficiency to perform and maintain effective and efficient search operational capability.

The purchasers or recipient of this textbook agrees to hold harmless the authors and contributors of this book. The authors and contributors take no responsibility for the use of this textbook or the information contained within. We are not responsible for or liable for statements made by instructors using this textbook.

This information serves as an introduction to basic aspects of search and rescue operations focusing on search operations. This is intended for the entry-level search responder to safely participate in SAR operations at the local level.

This information is based on the various American Society for Testing and Materials (ASTM) F32 Committee – Search and Rescue Standards for search and rescue. There are other standards such as National Fire Protection Association (NFPA) 1670 and 1006 that reference search and rescue that have been referenced. The AHJ and the reader need to be familiar with all applicable standards and policies and procedures.

First Edition – September 2019
Second Edition – October 2020
Third Edition – January 2022

Forward or Preface

Acknowledgment:

The Authors would like to extend a great appreciation to Dave Rogers, Retired Maryland Park Service Ranger who helped with the Land Navigation Chapter and taught the many Maryland Conservation Corps and the many Park Rangers and Maryland Department of Natural Resources personnel.

We would also like to thank the Maryland Department of Natural Resources Park Service for their dedication to the education of personnel in Search and Rescue at the Basic level so they know how to respond to a missing person incident in the Maryland Parks throughout Maryland.

Recognizing Past Pioneers of SAR:

The art and science of search and rescue management have exponentially progressed since the later 1960s and early 1970s. This progress was noted in Tim Setnicka's book "Wilderness Search and Rescue" when noted the contributions of Dennis Kelly, Jon Wartes, Bob Mattson, Bill, and Jean Syrotuck, Skip Stoffel, and Bill Wade on their work on Lost Person Behavior, Search Management, and Search Techniques. Today Robert Koester, Don Cooper, Jack Frost, Rick Button, and many others have brought searching for a missing and lost person closer to a scientific process and improving all the work that has been done to date from the late 1960s. The application of search management and use of lost person behavior especially in the law enforcement community and the local, county, and state parks has saved countless lives and given families closure.

About the Authors:

Michael J. Zabetakis – "Mike" – A lifelong resident of Maryland. He currently works as an electrical engineering technician for a Bio-Medical company. Michael started his Search and Rescue training in 2001, obtaining his team leader rating in 2002.

He progressed his training over the years to include Managing Land Search Operations at the University of Maryland Baltimore County (UMBC) in 2010 and has returned each year as a Field Training Advisor for the program. Michael currently has an Incident Commander rating in Civil Air Patrol (CAP) and Search Manager with the Maryland State Police Special Operations Division.

Serves as a primary SAR Management instructor for Law Enforcement in Maryland. Michael has been a staff member of the CAP National Emergency Services Academy, Ground Search and Rescue School since 2003 currently serving as the school Commandant.

Coleman P. Brown III – "Cole" – A lifelong resident of Maryland. He has been involved in Search and Rescue since 1980 and worked his way up through the process. He has served on the National Search and Rescue Association (NASAR) Board of Directors, Instructor for NASAR, and served on several committees. He served on the National Search and Rescue Committee's various working groups. He is an adjunct instructor at the University of Maryland Baltimore County for Search Management and Disaster Management. He also serves as an Instructor for Maryland State Police and the Maryland Department of Natural Resources Park Service for Search Management and the Foundation for Search Operations.

He is a Captain in the Civil Air Patrol serving as one of their Incident Commanders and on the National Geographic Information Systems (GIS) Team. He has been in the emergency services field as an Emergency Medical Technician, Fire Fighter, Fire Instructor, and Fire Officer for over 40 years.

Fulltime he has had a career as a Risk Control Engineer in the insurance risk management field for 32 years. He is a Certified Fire Protection Specialists (CFPS) with NFPA and is a Highly Protected Risk (HPR) Specialist.

Serving as Search Manager and Civilian Search Coordinator with the Maryland State Police Special Operations Division, he is a primary SAR Management instructor for Law Enforcement in Maryland.

Table of Contents

Appendixes

Table of Contents

Chapter 1. Basic Knowledge of Search and Rescue

Objectives:

1. Understanding and define the following terms: *ASTM F3098 (16) 11.1*
   a. Search
   b. Rescue
   c. Recovery
   d. Search and Rescue
2. Understand and describe the different types of Search Environments
   a. Terrain – Urban, Rural, Non-wilderness, or Wilderness
   b. Hazardous Areas – Water, Swiftwater, Cliffs, Etc.
3. Describe the difference between Search vs. Rescue
4. Describe the Search Operations Architecture and its components
5. Understanding the four core elements of a Search and Rescue Operations *ASTM F3098 (16) 11.1.4*
6. Understand, describe and know the six phases of search and rescue operations. *ASTM F3098 (16) 11.2*
7. Be aware of the standards and certifications available for Search and Rescue
8. Understand and be able to describe the search and rescue system and the roles of agencies or organizations at various levels which coordinate, provide resources and services, or perform other functions in search and rescue at the: *ASTM F3098 (16) 11.3*
   a. International and National
   b. State or Provincial
   c. County or Tribal
   d. Local

In this chapter Basic Knowledge of Search and Rescue, we will focus on the introduction and what is Search and Rescue.

American Standard for Testing and Materials (ASTM)

ASTM International, formerly known as the American Society for Testing and Materials, is an international standards organization that develops and publishes voluntary consensus technical standards for a wide range of materials, products, systems, and services. They were founded in 1898 and the headquarters is in West Conshohocken, PA. They have over 12,500 Standards.

This book is based on the American Standard for Testing and Materials (ASTM) Standard **ASTM F3098-16** - Standard Guide for Training of Non-Wilderness Land Search Team Member.

ASTM Committee F32 on Search and Rescue was formed in 1988. F32 currently has 80 members participating on 3 technical subcommittees that are responsible for 65 approved standards. The committee promotes knowledge and the development of standards (classifications, guides, practices, specifications, terminology, and test methods) for search and rescue activities.

Three sub-committees work on standard development:
    F32.01 Equipment, Testing, and Maintenance
    F32.02 Management and Operations
    F32.03 Personnel, Training, and Education

The committee meets in November in conjunction with the International Tech Rescue Symposium (ITRS) with approximately 20 members participating in one to two days of technical meetings. F32 Committee standards are published in Volume 13.02 of the Annual Book of ASTM Standards. These standards are voluntary but are international standards.

Organizations such as the National Association for Search and Rescue (NASAR) have adopted these standards for their courses and certification programs as well as many jurisdictions throughout the United States.

When considering a program such as search and rescue it requires a standard, a training course, and then a certification process. This is to ensure that the objectives are met to ensure that a search meets the proficiency of the knowledge, skills, and abilities based on the written standard. The certification process allows the searcher to be tested based on what they have learned.

National Fire Protection Association (NFPA)

National Fire Protection Association (NFPA) is an international non-profit organization that delivers information and knowledge through various research projects and various consensus codes and standards. They have standards that affect search and rescue operations and personnel, especially in the fire and rescue services. Two of those are outlined below and are comparable to ASTM.

NFPA 1670 – Standard on Operations and Training for Technical Search and Rescue Incidents - The standard identifies and establishes levels of functional capability for efficiently and effectively conducting technical search and rescue operations at incidents.

NFPA 1006 – Standard for Technical Rescue Personnel Professional Qualifications – It identifies the minimum Job Performance Requirements (JPRs) for performing Technical Rescue Operations which may occur on a missing person search once found.

It is important to understand and be aware of the various standards. Why are standards necessary? Because a life is on the line and the standards help ensure that each search runs consistently and follows best practices for the best outcome. Additionally, it ensures the safety of the many professionals that are conducting the search which includes you.

Intention and Scope of this Course and Book

This is an introductory level textbook for the entry-level SAR provider in a Non-Wilderness Environment and searching for and is prepared for a period not longer than 12hrs at a time. This course is set up to provide the knowledge and limited skills to conduct search operations. This course focuses on the knowledge in a classroom setting for 16 hours and the students are tested on that knowledge.

This text and course focus on the aspect of Searching for a missing person and the rescue component will be handled by the local fire and rescue services which may include Sheriff's Search and Rescue Teams, Rescue Squads, and other Search and Rescue Teams pre-established in the jurisdiction having authority (JHA).

This course will not qualify you to work around helicopters even though we talk about the use of helicopters in search operations. A separate course for helicopter safety, helicopter search operations, and orientation to helicopter operations will be needed for working around or riding in a helicopter. Each helicopter is different and each jurisdiction or agency that has a helicopter system will be different with its procedures.

This course will not qualify you to participate in Swiftwater search and rescue operations but will cover safety precautions and procedures to be employed when working around still or swift water in the search area of operation. When working near Swiftwater it is practical for each SAR Provider to wear the appropriate Personal Flotation Device (PFD). There are many dangers associated with Swiftwater which requires special training to work in that environment.

This course also does not determine your personal medical or physical fitness for conducting searches. A SAR Provider will have to determine the requirement for personal fitness for their search team, organization, and jurisdiction before being approved to respond to a search. SAR Providers should demonstrate annually that they meet both the medical and physical fitness requirements for their team, organization, or AHJ. Some organizations follow the physical performance requirements as outlined in the United States Forest Service for wildland firefighters NWCG PMS 307.

Understanding the Difference between Wilderness and Non-Wilderness Environments:

Defining the Wilderness and Non-wilderness environments is critical for a search team member.

Wilderness or wildland is a natural environment on Earth that has not been significantly modified by human activity. Defining wilderness or wildland is, "The most intact, undisturbed wild natural areas left on our planet—those last truly wild places that humans do not control and have not developed with roads, pipelines or other industrial infrastructure." ["What is a Wilderness Area". The WILD Foundation. Archived from the original on 4 December 2012. Retrieved 20 February 2009.]

The Wilderness Act defines wilderness as "an area where the earth and its community of life are untrammeled by man, where man himself is a visitor who does not remain."

The non-wilderness environment is an area of land which has been developed from parks with trails created by man, lands that have been timbered or occupied or modified by man to the urban environments.

Non-wilderness, n—an area located within, or immediately next to, urban boundaries, no further than 0.5 miles (0.8 kilometers) from a road readily accessible by emergency personnel, and which may include parks, wild areas, private, state, and municipal lands. [ASTM 3098 – 16]

Non-technical terrain - tract of land characterized by minimal slopes and little variation in elevation, where a person can move safely and effectively on two feet, without handholds, and without the need for a belay. [ASTM F2751-16]

Mountainous environments - mountainous terrain, n—a tract of land characterized by steep slopes and great variations in elevation, where the ability to negotiate routes based on the Yosemite Decimal System rated Class 2–4, and occasionally Class 5, is required, and where travel is limited by steep to vertical rock, steep forested or brush-covered terrain, talus slopes, boulder fields, and occasional snow and/or ice obstacles.

Be mindful of the environment in which you are capable of working within because if not, you can get yourself into trouble. The Non-Wilderness Land Search Team Member is an entry-level position. This is an introductory level course giving the Non-Wilderness Land Search Team Member awareness of the entire search and rescue overview, but work is conducted in a non-wilderness and non-technical environment with a focus on search operations.

Search, Rescue, and Recovery:

Search, Rescue, and Recovery involves a variety of emergency first responders from law enforcement and sheriff, natural resources police, national, state, and local park services, fire and rescue, and volunteer search and rescue teams. A search operation involves law enforcement officers conducting the investigation and conducting search management, K9s and their handlers, ground search team members, helicopter crews, equestrian teams, mantrackers, rescue and medical personnel, and others. Typically, this is a single jurisdiction but multiple agency search.

Now to define Search and Rescue which is normally referred to and abbreviated as "SAR". This term is used to describe an incident during which we look for and evacuate a lost or overdue subject. The term SAR describes two distinct functions;

1. **Search** – an operation using available resources to locate persons in distress.

2. **Rescue** – an operation using available resources to retrieve persons in distress, provide for their initial medical considerations and transport them to a safe environment.

Search	Rescue
Search is to identify and locate persons who are or may become distressed or injured and are unable to return to a place of safety on their own.	Rescue is to access, stabilize, and evacuate distressed or injured persons, by whatever means necessary, to ensure their timely transfer to an appropriate care facility or to a familiar environment.

Most search and rescue incidents are closely associated with outdoor activities and in the outdoor environment. However, SAR and more specifically the function of search do regularly occur in a rural or urban setting. Search and rescue can and will occur during disasters such as hurricanes, flooding events, earthquakes, wind storms (tornados), forest fires, or terrorist attacks. These disaster search and rescue events require specialized training and will not be addressed in this training.

In many jurisdictions in the United States, search for a missing person is conducted by the law enforcement agency of that jurisdiction. While the rescue function will normally be conducted by the fire and rescue organizations in that jurisdiction. There are jurisdictions in the Western United States in which the sheriff has full jurisdiction over search and rescue. The National Park Service manages millions of square miles of land and is the authority having jurisdiction and will conduct and be responsible for search and rescue within their jurisdiction.

The term search and rescue does denote two separate functions. Even though we hope that every search will end in a successful rescue there are times where the missing subject has succumbed to their injuries or the environment and are deceased. The term **recovery** is the function of retrieving a body of a fatality after they have been located.

Defining Search and Rescue as a whole is the employment of available personnel and facilities to find and render aid to persons and properties in distress or potential distress in air, water, or land. Air can be further defined as anything suspended in air and in space such as our astronauts on the International Space Station or traveling to or on a planet. Water involves Swiftwater, on the surface of water and underwater. Most of what we will focus on is on the ground.

When combining the terms search and rescue together an example of one state's statue of the definition of search and rescue is:

> *"Search and rescue means the acts of searching for, rescuing, or recovering by the means of ground, marine, or air activity any person who becomes lost, injured, or is killed while outdoors as a result of a natural or man-made disaster including instances involving searches for downed or missing aircraft."*

Understanding the Importance of Search Management

Three critical elements will influence the success of a large search: the coordination and use of proper resources, the strategy, and tactics but most critically is management. Successful search missions are dependent on a quick response, detailed interview, efficient searching, and good management. Good management is using the most appropriate and efficient resources in the right order to find the missing subject. Anything less than this could be called *"Negligence"*.

As a search and rescue professional you need to be as prepared as possible for the search and rescue operations and be ready. The most critical component is search management and the search manager who will manage the resources, investigate the situation, determine and develop the strategy and initiate the tactics through the various type of resources.

Search management requires specialized training and experience and is handled by a qualified search manager from the jurisdiction law enforcement agency. Good search management will ensure that you the SAR Provider are searching in the right place based on the size of the search area and the time allocated to search the area assigned. Resources with the right strategy and implementing the right tactics based on the strategy within a defined search area with appropriate allotted time should result in a successful search of clearing an area or finding this missing subject.

Resources: Can be equipment, material, or people. People that are trained and experienced are searchers that are equipped and prepared (trained properly) to search in various areas. Equipment can be tools (stokes basket, tracking stick, K9's, Equines, ready packs, or 24 hr. Packs, rescue gear, GPS units, visual enhancing items (binoculars or handheld thermal imagers), or other items. Materials can include maps, task assignments, pictures, or other materials to aid in the search task. For all of this to work requires a SAR Manager who knows how the resource capabilities, where to get the resources, and how to deploy the resource.

Strategy: The SAR Provider must know the fundamentals of search theory and principles to develop sound task objectives. While the Search Manager needs to understand the same but for establishing the overall incident objectives. This is known as the planning phase for the task for the Searcher or the entire incident for the Search Manager.

Tactics: The Search manager needs to develop an adequate plan for applying the proper resources in the most appropriate locations at the right time and in the right order to efficiently and effectively meet the objectives. While the SAR Provider develops a plan for accomplishing the task of their search area effectively and efficiently to meet the task-specific objective.

Your focus during a search should be on the missing person. When working on a search and rescue incident we are always working for the missing person. Below is a quote from Lieut. Col. Robert Mattson United States Air Force commander of the AFRCC in the early 1970s.

"You dedicate hours of your time and much money for SAR. But, who are you (really) working for? I'll give you some help. You're not working for the Air Force, ... your unit commander, the emergency services officer, the state, the sheriff, the FBI, your family, nor even yourself. If you think you are working for one of these, you are in the wrong business! You have only one person who really matters on a SAR mission, and that person is the potential survivor. I use the word "Potential" because if you don't work for the survivors, they may never be saved."

Most wilderness emergencies including missing person searches are normally solved by the victim or outside help within 72 hours. The decisions and actions taken by the responsible authority during the first six (6) hours are the most critical influencing the overall outcome.

SUCCESS FAST
the ultimate objective

Search Operations Architecture

There are four critical areas of Search Operations and a successful search will ensure that each area is covered. This structure or architecture covers the 4 critical areas that will influence the overall outcome of the search operation.

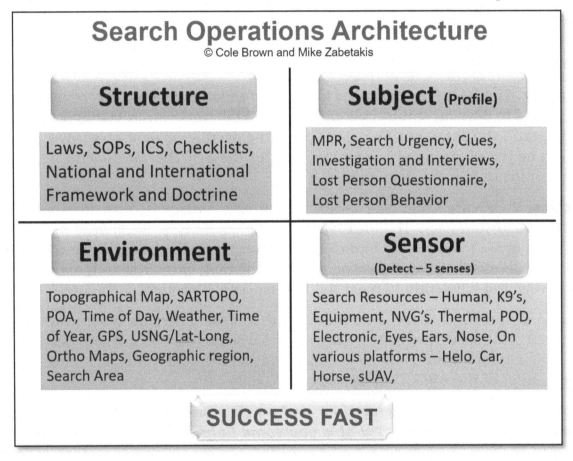

One of the Sensors is the SAR Provider and an additional sensor can be added to enhance the search capabilities. Understanding the environment and how the subject interacts and behaves within that environment is important. But all of this is down within a structure. There is an intertwined interaction between these four critical areas.

Four Core Elements of SAR:

The four core elements of search and rescue, also known as the acronym **LAST**. **LAST** stands for **L**ocate, **A**ccess, **S**tabilize, and **T**ransport. The operations proceed through this four-phase process. This was first identified in Tim Setnicka's book, Wilderness Search and Rescue. Locate is the function of *search*, while access, stabilize, and transport is the function of *rescue*. This is based on the timeline in this continuous cycle. The most critical component through any search operations is ensuring that there is an effective law enforcement investigation from the beginning and throughout the search. A search without an effective investigation will be difficult and fruitless. The investigation will determine the starting point, the situation why the person is missing, and the initial search area.

Locate represents the act of searching for and finding the subject in need of rescue. This requires that responders have the skills needed to go out and find overdue or lost or missing subjects as well as survive and function in that same environment so as not to become a liability or part of the problem. This is usually the longest and most difficult phase of the search effort. Finding a person in an urban, suburban, or wilderness environment all pose various particular challenges. The "Locate" phase of the response should prioritize its efforts on distinguishing or finding relevant clues to locate the subject.

Access represents the phase of gaining a safe approach to access the subject once they have been located. There have been many occasions in which the location of the subject has been established, however gaining access to them may be delayed due to various external factors. The subject may signal using a flare, a mirror, smoke, or some other method. But, due to terrain characteristics, it may take hours or days for a rescue team to hike to the subject. Priority during this phase should be focused on rescuer safety. The searchers should not develop tunnel vision when they locate the subject and are in a hurry to get to the subject jeopardizing their personal safety.

Stabilize represents the phase in which the rescuer focuses their efforts on maintaining the physical and mental well-being of the subject until the patient can be transferred to a safe environment. This may include providing medical attention such as basic first aid to advanced life support. It may just involve emotional support or food and water so that they may be able to be assisted by the rescuers by walking out of the environment on their abilities under the supervision of the rescuers. In most parts of the United States, search teams have a medically trained member on each crew or task assignment. Regardless of medical training, we need to be able to recognize the subject's medical and rescue requirements and have the ability to request the additional resources required for the patient's needs.

Transport is the phase, which requires moving the patient from where they were found to a safe location or an appropriate care facility. There are many types of transportation available ranging from carrying a victim out in a litter to ATVs and helicopters or riding out on a trained equine team. The rescuer will need to understand the requirements to safely and efficiently accomplish the task of transporting the patient to safety.

The Missing subject may or may not be injured, but if no one acts, and injury or death may occur. Some type of action is necessary.

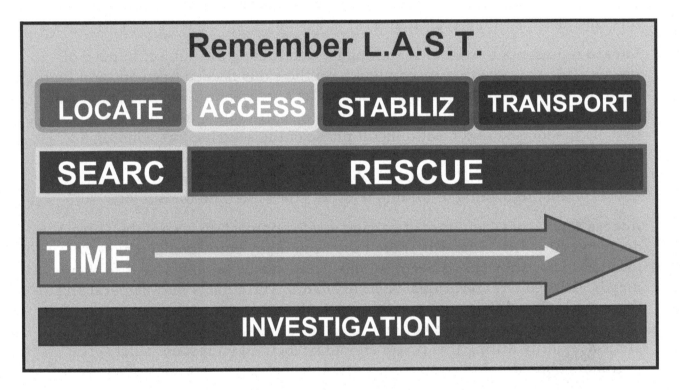

Search incidents occur in many forms, many incidents may last a short time while other incidents may last several days. Search incidents may be simple to plan and organize or can be complex involving an incident management team, several search managers, and hundreds of searchers looking for the missing subject for days. Due to the complexity of these incidents, it takes detailed and appropriate planning and implementation of strategies and tactics to ensure we are searching in the right area with the right resource to find that missing person.

Six Phases of a Search and Rescue Operation:

Search missions no matter how simple or complex have six basic components which the incident will follow and their order of occurrence is almost always constant. These components ensure that it is a continuous cycle allowing us to continuously improve and do better on each search. A further detailed review of these components can be found in Chapter 9 - Tactical Search Operations

- Preplanning – Occurs before the incident.
- Notification – Notifying personnel of a problem
- Planning and Strategy – Gathering information, assessing the problem.
- Tactics and Operations – Determining the solution and acting on it.
- Suspension – Objective is located or if not, operations suspended
- Demobilization – Restoring people, materials, and equipment to a ready state.
- Critique – an evaluation of the entire incident and all components.

Besides the incident and management going through these components the SAR Provider will go through these personally preparing themselves both mentally and physically and critiquing themselves if they can do better the next time through training, practice, and preparation.

SAR Components

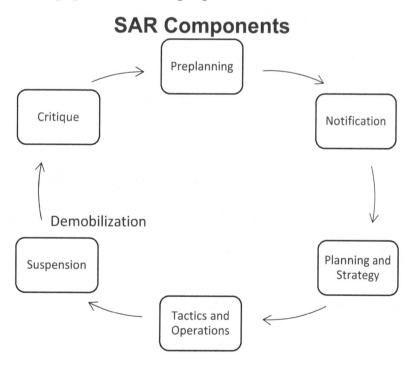

Preplanning is looking at the response area and identifying potential SAR problems and developing preventative search and rescue activities for citizens and kids like the Hug a Tree Program.

The Anatomy of Search and Rescue:

When combining the Components of SAR outlined above with the Search and Rescue Phases of **LAST** we can show in a flow chart or a process the entire Anatomy of Search and Rescue and the continuous cycle of improvement. Utilizing the trained search managers using National Incident Management System and the Incident Command System will ensure effective and efficiently run search operations with the ultimate goal of finding the missing person quickly. **SUCCESS FAST!**

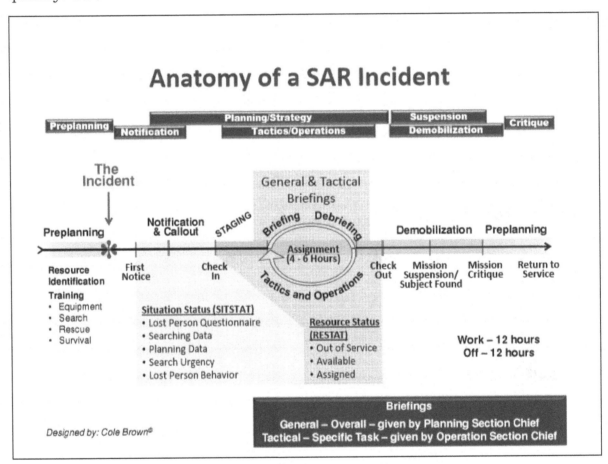

Legal and Ethical Aspects of SAR

Some legal issues applicable to the provision of emergency care are so important that they are considered essential knowledge for all SAR personnel. Although a comprehensive overview of legal issues related to SAR cannot be provided here, some of the most important issues related to emergency services personnel will be reviewed in the context of search and rescue. Search and rescue organizations and personnel have a responsibility to seek competent legal counsel when questions arise.

Standard of Care

All rescue personnel is required by law to act or behave toward others in a certain way regardless of the activity involved. Depending on the situation, one may have a duty to either act or not act. How one acts or behaves is called a standard of care.

Several factors influence the standard of care and therefore the appropriateness of one's conduct. Local customs, statutes, ordinances, regulations, and professional and institutional standards all have a bearing on the measure of one's actions.

Developing and implementing written policies and procedures for search operations and how SAR Providers should respond and act will become part of the standard of care for your organization through the training and planning.

Negligence

The outcome of even the best-run SAR incident is always unpredictable. Unfortunately, the subject of a SAR incident can allege that the care rendered, or the rescue performed, was improper, inadequate, or negligent. Negligence is the failure to provide the same care someone with similar training and in a similar situation would provide.

To determine negligence the following four factors must be present:

1. **Duty** – The rescuer had a duty to act reasonably within his or her training.
2. **Breach of Duty –** The rescuer failed to perform that duty and did not act within the accepted and reasonable standard of care.
3. **Damages** – The subject was injured or harmed.
4. **Causes** – the rescuer's failure was the cause of the subject's injury or loss.

The heavy burden to prove these four requirements is a strong deterrent against frivolous and unjustified lawsuits.

A prudent and reasonable SAR Provider in a SAR event needs to simply act in accordance with their level of training and meet applicable standards such as NFPA and ASTM and the policies and procedures set by the AHJ and their organization.

Other legal issues that may arise are Abandonment, Confidentiality of mission information, HIPPA, talking to the media, social media, and entering on private property. Each of these items should be addressed at the team level. Working with or for a law enforcement agency will assist but not alleviate responsibility.

National and International SAR System

Internationally, two primary conventions govern international search and rescue:
- International Maritime Organization (IMO) document on the international convention on maritime search and rescue (1979)
- International Civil Aviation Organization (ICAO) document on the convention on international civil aviation (1949) Annex 12 (search and rescue).

There are several international treaties and agreements that will apply to civil SAR within the US and with neighboring countries. The primary international convention of interest to land search and rescue authorities is the convention on international civil aviation (Annex 12 – search and rescue) applies to persons in distress in both domestic and international flights.

ICAO and IMO both work together to establish The International Aeronautical Maritime Search and Rescue (IAMSAR) Manual which provides guidance on aeronautical and maritime search and rescue applicable both internationally and nationally.

There are three volumes to the IAMSAR manual:

Volume 1 (organization and management)
volume 2 (mission coordination)
volume 3 (mobile facilities)

The National SAR Plan

The United States and the various federal cabinet-level interagency partners for search and rescue have established the national Search Rescue Plan (NSP) for the United States. It describes how the U.S. will meet its international legal and humanitarian obligations to provide search and rescue services. It establishes over-arching federal SAR policy, assigned SAR responsibilities to federal agencies, and adopts the IAMSAR Manual and the National Search and Rescue Supplement (NSS) for use by the US Search and Rescue Agencies.

IMO and ICAO are primarily responsible for international maritime and aviation safety and security. Both organizations continue to foster close SAR cooperation between themselves, nations, and maritime and aeronautical SAR authorities and industry stakeholders to standardize and harmonize SAR services worldwide

National SAR supplement (NSS)

The NSS, which is the bridge between IAMSR Manual and The National Search Rescue Plan. These documents can be found on the US Coast Guard.

National Search And Rescue Committee (NSARC) – is responsible for coordinating in improving federal involvement in civil search and rescue for aeronautical, maritime, and land operations within the United States. A list of the federal NSARC member agencies are listed below:

The Land Search and Rescue Addendum

The Land Search and Rescue Addendum is an important manual in this generalization of land-based SAR operations. Information in this publication was compiled from many sources and took into account decades of SAR best practices, as well as lessons learned from tragedies, mishaps, and successes. It is also the foundational resource for the national search and rescue committee on identifying key agencies and organizations that support land-based SAR operations. It provides guidance on how to plan and organize the implementation of SAR operations.

Federal, State, and Local Coordination for Search and Rescue

There are two federal agencies that have direct coordinating functions for search and rescue in the United States. The United States Air Force (USAF) and the United States Coast Guard (USCG) have direct coordinating functions for search and rescue.

U.S. Air Force

The United States Air Force serves as the inland search and rescue coordinator responsible for search and rescue within the United States. Within this agency, The Air Force Rescue Coordination Center (AFRCC) is responsible for coordinating search and rescue. The AFRCC serves as this agency responsible for coordinating inland federal SAR activities within the 48 contiguous United States along with Alaska and Hawaii, while also providing SAR assistance to Mexico and Canada.

AFRCC is directly tied into the Federal Aviation Administration's alerting system and the U.S. Mission Control Center. In addition to the Search and Rescue Satellite Aided Tracking (SARSAT) information, the AFRCC computer system contains resource files that list federal and state organizations, which can conduct or assist in SAR efforts throughout North America. The center operates 24 hours a day seven days a week and is located at Tyndall Air Force Base, Panama City, Florida.

When a distress call is received, the center investigates the request, coordinates with federal, state, and local officials, and determines the type and scope of response necessary. Once verified as an actual distress situation, the AFRCC requests support from the appropriate federal SAR force. This may include Civil Air Patrol, U.S. Coast Guard, or other Department of Defense assets, as needed.

AFRCC will process two of the three Search and Rescue Satellite Aided Tracking devices being an Emergency Locator Transmitter (ELT) located within a general aviation airplane and a Personal Locating Beacon (PLB) typically carried by a person such as a hiker or a boater.

The AFRCC also has a responsibility for coordinating with each of the 48 states on how those states would like search and rescue to be conducted for aeronautical and land searching within their state. This is conducted through Memorandums of Agreement (MOA) between 1st. Air Force (AFNORTH) and the state governors. Based on the Memorandums of Agreement (MOA) A Memorandum of Understanding (MOU) between the state agency assigned by the governor to handle search and rescue for aeronautical and land search is developed between that state agency and the AFRCC.

The United States Air Force has a civilian auxiliary known as the Civil Air Patrol. See below for more details on the Civil Air Patrol and its mission.

United States Coast Guard (USCG)

The United States Coast Guard is responsible for search and rescue within all navigable waterways within the United States. USCG operates under the Department of Homeland Security (DHS), is a federal SAR Coordinator of the United States Aeronautical and Maritime Search and Rescue Regions (SRR). They provide direct support for air, ship, boat, and response team operations.

The United States Coast Guard also is the sponsor and chair of the National Search and Rescue Committee which oversees the National Search and Rescue System and US involvement in International Search and Rescue.

Federal Aviation Administration (FAA)

The FAA, operating under the Department of Transportation (DOT), through Its Air Route Traffic Control Centers (ARTCC) and Flight Service Stations (FSS), monitors in-flight – follows aircraft and maybe the first agency to alert and RCC of an aviation emergency or overdue aircraft.

Once alerting, the RCC and the FAA work together to locate the aircraft, reviewing radio communications, (if available) and radar data to ascertain as closely as possible a good last known position (LKP). Concurrently, other FA facilities conduct "ramp" checks at airports where an aircraft may have landed.

The FAA can recall recorded radar data and identify and trace aircraft that are at sufficient altitude to be tracked by radar. RCCs can seek this radar data from the FAA, which can greatly assist in aircraft searches, as well as providing route and last radar position data.

Most aircraft are required by the FAA to carry an Emergency Locator Transmitter's (ELT's) that are designed to automatically activate an event of an accident.

Pilots may also file a flight plan which is information about their intended route and airports that they are taking off from and landing. This information is invaluable to search and rescue in the planning and executing of their search efforts.

Civil Air Patrol (CAP) - United States Air Force Auxiliary

The Civil Air Patrol (CAP) is a congressionally chartered, nonprofit organization of experienced aviation–trained volunteers located in every state and Puerto Rico that also serves as the United States Air Force Auxiliary.

CAP has the largest number of light civil aircraft that have land-based SAR and other capabilities including specialized sensors for direction finding and airborne digital imaging. They also have the largest number of small UASs within the United States. They also have a GIS Team that supports FEMA during National Emergencies. CAP also operates a nationwide communication system in support of its air and ground operations. They are a private nonprofit, 501(c)(3) Corporation and auxiliary of the United States Air Force. CAP headquarters is at Maxwell Air Force Base, Alabama. They are committed to aviation safety and emergency response.

Civil Air Patrol was established on December 1, 1941, and has three congressionally mandated missions:
- Aerospace Education Safety
- Cadet Programs
- Emergency Services

State Search and Rescue Authorities

State authorities have more of a coordinating role working with the County, City, or local jurisdictions. They may also be involved in legislative or policy for search and rescue. Some states will have a direct role with their emergency management agency or their state police or law enforcement agency. Some state agencies will also be setting the criteria for standards for teams.

Local Search and Rescue Authorities

The backbone of the search and rescue system resides at the County, City, and local levels where teams are working with the local law enforcement agencies or emergency management agencies. A lot of SAR Teams are non-profit organizations that provide a service to the local agencies.

Responsible Authority:

It is very important to understand who you or your agency is working for and who has overall responsibility for the incident. Most SAR Providers belong to a volunteer or non-paid professional search and rescue team or are part of a law enforcement auxiliary and maybe a fire or rescue first responder.

The Responsible Authority is the government agency or agencies that may have legal responsibility for finding missing persons and has jurisdiction over the area where the person becomes missing.

Due to the potential criminal nature of a missing person's search and rescue operations, the responsible authority is the Law Enforcement Agency of that jurisdiction. Why? Because of the criminal potential of the incident to end up as a homicide, suicide, or abduction along with other criminal aspects of the case of why the person went missing.

Remember:
As long as the **Classical Mystery** is involved a law enforcement agency should be in charge and should remain in charge to maintain the continuity of the chain of evidence.

Chapter 2 – The Searcher

Outline:

- Personal Safety
- Four Components of Physical Fitness
- Qualities of a SAR Individual - Six Expected Traits
- Physical Demands on a Searchers
- Gear, Clothing, and Personal Safety
- Searcher Attitude

Objectives:

1. List and be able to describe the Six Expected qualities of a Search and Rescue Provider
2. Understand and describe the searcher attitude and the philosophy of Serving others.
3. Understand what it means to be physically and mentally prepared.
4. List and describe the four components of fitness and the importance of Personal Fitness. *ASTM F3098 (16) 5*
5. Be able to describe various other certifications that a searcher may need before becoming operational. *ASTM F3098 (16) 6.1, 6.2, 6.3, 7.5,*
6. Be able to discuss how to protect yourself as a searcher from the effects of the environment *ASTM F3098 (16) 7.1.2*
7. Be able to describe the appropriate searcher attire and pack for food, water, and survival. *ASTM F3098 (16) 7.2, 9.1.1*
8. Understand the type and use of the Personal protective equipment needed to safely participate in search operations. *ASTM F3098 (16) 7.8, 9.1*

Personal Safety

SAR may be a collateral duty for many. This may not be your full-time duty or assignment. As a volunteer, you commit a significant amount of time and financial commitment. The commitment to being a SAR Team Volunteer is not easy and you can train for months if not years before you get on your first search operations.

The safety of searchers and their teammates is critical. It does the missing person no good if the search is delayed because a team member is not prepared and becomes lost, sick, or injured. We will focus on getting you, the searcher, mentally and physically prepared for search operations.

Staying found and knowing where you are critically important and later in the book, we will talk about land navigation. The most important aspect is always using the buddy system and never going alone. The buddy system or team concept is to ensure each team member looks after one another.

Having a dual communication system with the command post is also an important safety factor ensuring the ability to communicate information and the ability to notify if an emergency arises with the team. This can be a portable radio or a cell phone. Having a GPS and remote tracking capabilities will also ensure your whereabouts. Survival is not part of the entry-level position and will not be discussed in this book. It is always good to take a survival class and in more advanced classes in search and rescue survival is required.

> *Having a mindset of safety and survival should be everyone's job.*

Four Components of Physical Fitness

The searcher should focus on preparing themselves physically by focusing on four components of total overall fitness (remember the acronym – **SAFE**):

- **Strength** – The ability to exert force on physical objects using muscles. Strength can be divided into 2 categories Short-term endurance and long-term endurance
- **Agility** – The ability to successfully change the body's direction efficiently, using a combination of coordination, speed, and strength.
- **Flexibility** – the ability to adapt the body to different positions and under different circumstances. Stretching is essential before starting physical activities; it will also reduce musculoskeletal injuries.
- **Endurance** – is different than other forms of physical stress in that fatigue of the muscle and cardiovascular system do not force the effort to end. The need for sleep, build-up of non-recyclable body waste chemicals, depletion of energy stores, psychological failure, or achieving the goal will bring the effort to an end.

Qualities of the SAR Individual

The SAR workers must understand exactly what is expected by managers and leaders. As a helpful tool to remember these key guidelines, the acronym "PHACKS" was devised to convey these expectations. SAR workers should use these guidelines when attempting to exhibit the qualities necessary to become a team player in the field.

Acronym "PHACKS":

- **"P" – Proficient** - Performing with expert correctness and Competency. Being adept and proficient at what you do.
- **"H" – Humble** - Being unpretentious and modest identifying one's shortcomings.
- **"A" – Able** - Capable of performing, both physically and mentally
- **"C" – Competent** - The ability to perform a task.
- **"K" – Knowledgeable** - Familiarity, awareness, or understanding gained through formal study and experience.
- **"S" – Solicitous** - Full of polite concern for the well-being of others; Marked by or given to anxious care and often hovering attentiveness.

Attributes of Mental Fitness

There are four components to mental fitness and they will weigh heavy and if not in balance or in-check can cause you to not focus on the task at hand. They are:

1. **Emotional** – The ability to manage your emotions and be resilient.
2. **Social** – good relationships at work, home, and with your teammates.
3. **Financial** – feeling in control of finances and not stressed over finances
4. **Physical** - Mental and physical fitness and health are intertwined.

Attributes of Mental Fitness include –

- Be thorough
- Be confident and willing to learn
- Be conscientious
- Be assertive
- Be a team player

Training and Certifications:

A Searcher will need to obtain and maintain training or certifications in CPR and First aid, hazardous materials awareness, blood-borne pathogens, or rescue operations. Training such as this will ensure that you can provide first aid to your teammates or the missing subject.

If you perform CPR or First aid on a teammate or the missing subject, you need to ensure the protection of yourself and your teammates from bodily fluids or containments by knowing the dangers of an airborne and bloodborne pathogen. Understanding how to mitigate the risks requires knowledge of the types of pathogens and methods of transmission.

Also, mitigating the risk includes body substance isolation methods and personal protective equipment (PPE) such as rubber gloves and facemasks.

Depending on the condition and environment of where you may be searching it may lead you to a hazardous environment. Like a landfill or a swamp. Being aware of the hazardous environment and being able to identify it and communicate it to command correctly will ensure the safety of your team and yourself. Having hazardous materials awareness level training can assist in this situation.

The searcher needs to understand the minimum knowledge, skills, and abilities that a searcher must perform in a non-wilderness environment. The Searchers organization or the Authority Having Jurisdiction shall determine the depth or detail of the training required to meet the minimum Non-Wilderness Land Search Team member requirements. The Searcher should be able to demonstrate the skills learned at the end of the course. There should also be a clear understanding for practicing the skills and demonstrating the proficiency of the skills but the knowledge also. There may be a recertification requirement or a demonstration of skill proficiency. Some jurisdictions or organizations have either an annual or every three-year requirement.

Organizations and/or Authority Having Jurisdiction has the responsibility to establish guidelines for minimum standards of training for the Non-Wilderness Land Search Team Member and may set criteria for Trainee, Probationary, and Operational members.

The searcher should be prepared to demonstrate that they are physically capable of conducting a search in the environment within which they will work within their jurisdiction. This may include a minimum physical performance test or a work capacity test. The National Wildfire Coordinating Group (NWCG) has a document NWCG PMS 307 "Work Capacity Testing for Wildland Firefighters" and various other jurisdictions have similar testing requirements. This is to ensure the searcher is physically fit to perform the duties necessary without creating a hazard for other members of their team.

It is necessary to conduct a self-evaluation of your physical and mental capabilities to ensure that you will be an effective team member.

The searchers' organization or Authority Having Jurisdiction may require team members to demonstrate annually that they meet the requirements by completing a medical fitness, physical performance, or other tests to ensure they are healthy and capable of performing the tasks.

Physical Demands on a Searcher:

Search operations can include searching in densely wooded environments that can be extremely cold or hot depending on the season and wet or dry depending on the weather for 4 or more hours. Most of the work is walking on uneven surfaces for miles at varying elevations of a difference from 30 to 500 feet change in elevation. Time on a search can be as little as 2 hours to many days. Expectations of a search task would be searching with a team of two or more in a 100-acre area for 4 to 6 hours.

NASAR'S SAR Academy has a module on SAR Physical Fitness. This module covers the physical demands, injury prevention, fitness training, rest, and nutrition along with information on developing a fitness program for your team.

Gear and Personal Safety:

It is critical to carry water at least 2 liters of water to ensure you are properly hydrating during a search. Dehydration can sneak up on you quickly in both warm and cold weather environments. Lack of water or dehydration can decrease one's performance.

Energy levels within the body play an important role in warmth and performance. Having the appropriate type of food such as high-energy snacks ensures the body can perform at its peak especially during long searches.

Searchers are called out on very short time notification so it is critical to be prepared to respond by having a pack ready to go, called a **"ready pack"**. Most teams and jurisdictions require their team members to have sufficient clothing, gear, and food to sustain them in the field for at least 24 hours. A Non Wilderness search team member may only need enough to sustain them for 12 hours or less.

Wearing the appropriate clothing is critical. A police officer wearing a dress-type uniform or a firefighter wearing turnout gear is not the ideal clothing for the wilderness environment even during the colder season. Dress for the environment, hunting, and outdoor recreational clothing is a better option. Wearing appropriate hiking books with the right type of socks can keep your feet in good shape and warm during long hours of searching.

A searcher shall have and know how to use personal protective equipment (PPE) to safely participate in the field of a search operation. This would include the appropriate clothing, outwear, and personal field equipment. Having a durable and hands-free method of carrying the personal and survival gear and team equipment in a fanny pack or a backpack is necessary.

Items to consider for Clothing are:

Work Gloves
Hiking Boots
Headcover
Glove or Mittens
Sock and Sock Liners
Inner layers of basic and Long undergarments
Middle layers of warmth's Pants and Shirt
Outerwear for warmth and protection from wind and wetness (Top and Bottoms with Hood)
Rain gear
Always remember that cotton kills.

Gear items:

First aid kit
Eye Protection
Food and Water
Space Blanket
Pen, Pencil, and Paper
Safety Vest
Whistle
Compass
Signal Mirror
Light source – flashlight
Compass with 2-degree accuracy
Some type of multipurpose tool/Knife

The personal health, safety, and survival of the land search team member is critical to ensuring the success of the search operations. The safety of the searcher or/and the searchers teammates will allow them to focus their efforts on the task at hand.

Understanding what a searcher has to go through both mentally and physically will assist them in determining if they are cut out to be a searcher.

Due to the close proximity of resources and roads and a support system in a non-wilderness environment survival training is not provided. If the searcher is concerned with this it is recommended that they take a survival class so if they get separated from their team they can employ survival techniques as needed.

Searcher Attitude:

As a searcher you have to ask yourself the question, *"why do I want to do search and rescue?"*. Human beings, by their inherent nature, have always been willing to provide assistance and help to others who may be in distress. The Bible illustrates this when a shepherd left his entire herd of sheep to go find the single sheep that was lost. The U. S. Air Force pararescue and U. S. Coast Guard are two of the many military organizations that have coined the motto, **"so that others may live"**...

The willingness to place oneself self in harm's way and possibly sacrifice one's life in an attempt to save another is just one of those many traits found in the search and rescue environment. In Tim Setnicka's book *Wilderness Search and Rescue* the ideology of self-sacrifice and assistance to others has nurtured the development of many institutions devoted to helping others including rescue mountain travelers. In search and rescue, there is little to no financial compensation. Most people do search and rescue because of the inherent motivation of helping others. They also enjoy being in the outdoors, hiking, or working with friends or their four-legged companion the search dog or equine. Most search efforts in the United States today are based on volunteers which is the backbone of our searcher rescue system.

We find that searchers' personal lives may be sacrificed at times due to responding to a missing person search. A person should not get involved in search and rescue if they're looking for personal gain, fame, or fortune. Search and rescue is difficult to work requires long hours, physically demanding activities, and training, with emotional highs and lows and usually some financial sacrifices. A searcher needs to be prepared both mentally and physically.

> ### The Right Attitude is critical regarding your success in a search mission.

Searchers need to maintain a Positive Mental Attitude (PMA) and demonstrate a willingness to help regardless of the task to be successful.

Chapter 3 –Incident Command System – National Incident Management System.

- NIMS, FEMA, and Department of Homeland Security
- Homeland Security Presidential Directive
- Incident Command System Basics
  - Characteristics of the ICS
  - Command Staff
  - General Staff
  - 5 Major Functional Areas

Upon completion of this chapter and the related course activities, the student will be able to meet the following objectives:

- Understand why it is important to complete the National Incident Management System (NIMS) course IS-100, "Introduction to Incident Command System". *ASTM F3098 – 6.1 & 6.6.*
- Identify the four characteristics of an Incident Command System.
- Describe the five functional areas of the Incident Command System.
- Describe the general responsibilities of the Command and General Staff.
- Explain the functions of the following Incident Facilities;
  a) Incident Command Post
  b) Staging Area
  c) Incident Base
  d) Helibase
  e) Helispot
- Understand Unity and Chain of Command.
- Describe the ICS forms that make up the "Incident Action Plan" (IAP)
- Be able to explain why and what is "Span of Control"

Familiarizing you with the Incident Command System (ICS) and the NIMS principles used to manage incidents. Preparing you to coordinate with response partners from all levels of government and the private sector.

This chapter will be a recap of the incident management system used for most search operations. Search operations can be complex coupled with the growing need for multi-agency and multi-functional involvement. As a result, we expect the student to have completed certain classes regarding the Incident Command System.

ASTM F3098 (16) - Training of Non-Wilderness Land Search Team Member outlines the requirement of completing training and utilizing the incident command system.

    6.1 – Complete ICS 100

    6.6 – Operate within the ICS system

ASTM F1422-08 (Reapproved 2014 but originated in 1992) - Standard Guide for Using the Incident Command System Framework in Managing Search and Rescue Operations outlines the use of and implementation of NIMS, ICS, and National Response Framework (NRF) requirements for search and rescue operations.

It is recommended that the students complete the following Federal Emergency Management Administration classes through FEMA's Emergency Management Institute online independent study courses via: https://training.fema.gov/emi

Recommended courses to be completed:

    IS-100.C: Introduction to the Incident Command System, ICS 100

    IS-200.C: Basic Incident Command System for Initial Response, ICS 200

    IS-700.B: An Introduction to the National Incident Management System

    IS-800.C: National Response Framework, an Introduction

The Incident Command System (ICS) is a systematic approach to the management of emergency incidents. The system is used by fire departments, emergency medical services, law enforcement agencies, search and rescue teams, and other first responders. The system is flexible and scalable to all types and sizes of incidents and events. ICS is the most effective, efficient, and economical system to manage a search operation. ICS is a management system. From this training, you will gain information that will help sharpen your management skills and better equip you to be a fully effective incident commander or other ICS function. The Incident Command System (ICS) is a fundamental element of incident management. The use of ICS provides standardization through consistent terminology and established organizational structures.

ICS is part of the National Incident Management System (NIMS). The National Incident Management System (NIMS) is a systematic, proactive approach to guide all levels of government, nongovernmental organizations (NGOs), and the private sector to work together to prevent, protect against, mitigate, respond to, and recover from the effects of incidents. NIMS provides a consistent foundation for all incidents, ranging from daily occurrences to incidents requiring a coordinated Federal response.

NIMS is organized into three major components:
- Resource Management
- Command and Coordination - including the Incident Command System
- Communications and Information Management

FEMA released the refreshed National Incident Management System (NIMS) doctrine on October 17, 2019. NIMS provides a common, nationwide approach to enable the whole community to work together to manage all threats and hazards. NIMS applies to all incidents, regardless of cause, size, location, or complexity.

The response protocols and structures described in the National Response Framework align with the National Incident Management System (NIMS).

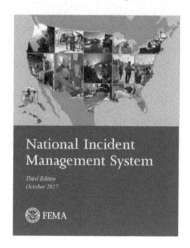

National Response Framework

Presidential Policy Directive / PPD-8 - **National Preparedness** is aimed at strengthening the security and resilience of the United States through systematic preparation for the threats that pose the greatest risk to the security of the nation, including acts of terrorism, cyber attacks, pandemics, and catastrophic natural disasters.

The **National Preparedness** System integrates efforts across the five preparedness mission areas—Prevention, Protection, Mitigation, Response, and Recovery—to achieve the goal of a secure and resilient Nation. The National Response Framework (NRF), part of the National Preparedness System, sets the strategy and doctrine for how the whole community builds, sustains, and delivers the Response core capabilities identified in the National Preparedness Goal in an integrated manner.

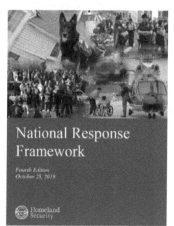

The National Response Framework (NFR) –defines the principles, roles, and structures that organize how we respond as a nation. The National Response Framework:
- describes how communities, tribes, states, the federal government, private-sectors, and nongovernmental partners work together to coordinate national response;

- describes specific authorities and best practices for managing incidents; and
- builds upon the National Incident Management System (NIMS), which provides a consistent template for managing incidents.

The priorities of response are to save lives, protect property and the environment, stabilize the incident, and provide for basic human needs. The following principles establish fundamental doctrine for the Response mission area: (1) engaged partnership, (2) tiered response, (3) scalable, flexible, and adaptable operational capabilities, (4) unity of effort through unified command, and (5) readiness to act.

The National Response Framework is built on the following five principles:
- Engaged partnership
- Tiered response
- Scalable, flexible, and adaptable operational capabilities
- Unity of effort through unified command
- Readiness to act.

The NRF is composed of a base document, Emergency Support Function (ESF) Annexes, and Support Annexes. The annexes provide detailed information to assist with the implementation of the NRF.
- ESF Annexes describe the Federal coordinating structures that group resources and capabilities into functional areas that are most frequently needed in a national response.
- Support Annexes describe the essential supporting processes and considerations that are most common to the majority of incidents.

There are 15 Emergency Support Function Annexes and 8 Support Annexes with individual documents designed to provide a concept of operations, procedures, and structures for achieving response directives for all partners in fulfilling their roles under the NRF. Now there are new **Lifelines** in the NRF.

Emergency Support Function (ESF) #9 – Search and Rescue (SAR) deploys Federal SAR resources to provide life-saving assistance to local, state, tribal, territorial, and insular area authorities, including local SAR Coordinators and Mission Coordinators, when there is an actual or anticipated request for Federal SAR assistance.

The Search and Rescue components:
- Structural Collapse (Urban) Search and Rescue (US&R)
- Waterborne Search and Rescue
- Inland/Wilderness Search and Rescue
- Aeronautical Search and Rescue

Background and History of the Incident Command System

In the 1970s with the problem of managing rapidly moving wildfires and managing multiple agencies doing multiple functions, it was determined that a management system was necessary. As a result, a committee known as FIRESCOPE (Firefighting Resources of California Organize for Potential Emergencies) identified the difficulties when responding to these wildfires:

- Too many people reporting to one supervisor.
- Different emergency response organizational structures.
- Lack of reliable incident information.
- Inadequate and incompatible communications.
- Lack of a structure for coordinated planning between agencies.
- Unclear lines of authority.
- Terminology differences between agencies.
- Unclear or unspecified incident objectives.

In the 1980s after ICS has been effectively used in managing wildfires made the transition into a national program under the Federal Emergency Management Agency's (FEMA) called the National Interagency Incident Management System (NIIMS). Over time there was such a need for the standardization of the ICS national training curriculum that the national wildfire coordinating group developed curriculum, training, position task-books, and instructor and student manuals. They also developed the ICS forms and glossary as part of the overall program.

After the September 11, 2001, terrorist attacks and the 2004 and 2005 hurricane seasons highlighted the need to focus on improving our emergency management, incident response capabilities, and coordination process across the country. There needed to be a comprehensive national approach applicable to all jurisdictional levels and across all functional disciplines, improves the effectiveness of emergency management/response personnel across a wide array of potential incidents and hazard scenarios. As of October 1, 2004, the Department of Homeland Security made funding contingent on the implementation and use of the Incident Command System for any agency including federal, state, and local agencies receiving federal funding.

Teamwork, collaboration, and cooperation are critical to the successful response. Key decision-makers who are represented at the incident command level help to ensure an effective response, the efficient use of resources, and responder safety. The adoption of NIMS demonstrated that there would be one Incident Management System for all agencies, specialties, and jurisdictions which would ensure efficient use of resources, communications, and overall management.

The Incident Command System

The Incident Command System must meet the following four characteristics in order to succeed:
- It must be organizationally **flexible** to expand and contract to meet the needs of the incident.
- It must be **efficient** to use on a day-to-day basis by all emergency response disciplines.
- It must use **common terminology** to allow personnel from various agencies and diverse geographic locations to meld rapidly into a common management structure.
- It must be **cost-effective**.

The Incident Command System (ICS) is based on the following 14 proven NIMS management characteristics, each of which contributes to the strength and efficiency of the overall system:

Characteristics of ICS

• Common Terminology	• Integrated Communications
• Modular Organization	• Establishment and Transfer of Command
• Management by Objectives	• Unified Command
• Incident Action Planning	• Chain of Command and Unity of Command
• Manageable Span of Control	• Accountability
• Incident Facilities and Locations	• Dispatch/Deployment
• Comprehensive Resource Management	• Information and Intelligence Management

The Five Major Functional Areas of the ICS

There are five functional areas in the Incident Command System which are:
1. Command
2. Operations
3. Planning
4. Logistics
5. Finance/Administration

The ICS organizational structure is modular, extending to incorporate all elements necessary for the type, size, scope, and complexity of the incident. It builds from the top down; responsibility and performance begin with the Incident Commander. As the need arises, four separate Sections can be used to organize the General Staff. If one individual can simultaneously manage all major functional areas, no further organization is required. If one or more of the functions require independent management, an individual is assigned responsibility for that function.

To maintain a manageable span of control the initial responding incident commander (IC) may determine it necessary to delegate functional management to one or more of the section chiefs. A section chief may establish branches, groups, divisions, or units, depending on the section. Similarly, each functional unit leader will further assign or delegate individual tasks within the unit, as needed.

For each organizational element, there is a title assigned along with various support positions.

ICS Organizational Elements

Organizational Element	Position Title	Support Position
Incident Commander	Incident Commander	Deputy
Command Staff	Officer	Assistant
Section	Section Chief	Deputy
Branch	Branch Director	Deputy
Division/Group	Supervisor	N/A
Strike Team/Task Force	Leader	Single Resource Boss, Companies/Crews
Unit	Unit Leader	Manager, Coordinator
Single Resource	Unit Designation	N/A
Technical Specialist	Specialist	N/A

Below is an overall Incident Command System chart is also known as an ICS 207. This shows the five major components of ICS: Incident Command, Operations, Planning, Logistics, and Finance/Administration.

Command – the Incident Commander (IC) is responsible for the overall management of the incident and therefore will establish the overall objectives for the incident. Although other functions may be left unfilled, there will always be an incident commander. Unfilled sections will normally be managed by the incident commander. As the demand for a section increases the incident commander will then delegate that responsibility to a section chief. The command can be Single, Unified, or Area Command.

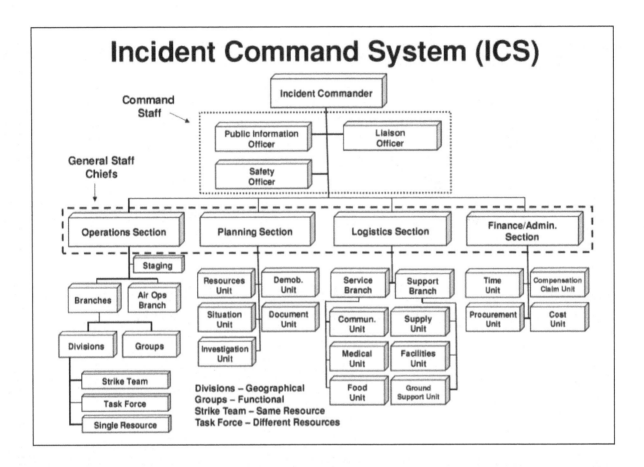

Incident Command System (ICS)

There are three types of incident command:

- **Single incident command** – this is the most common type of incident command. A single individual is designated as the incident commander and has sole responsibility for the entire incident.

- **Unified command** – unified command is often used for large incidents when multiple agencies are involved. Unified Command usually has one representative from each agency involved; these representatives act together as a single entity for command.

- **Area command** – during multiple incident situations, such as a large wildland fire or a natural disaster, an area command may be established. The area commanders provide for incident command at separate locations. In this case, they typically manage resources and do not establish objectives or develop IAP's (Incident Action Plans)

Operations – The Operation Section is responsible for directing and managing all incident tactical activities to meet the incident objectives in the Incident Action Plan (IAP). They implement all planned tactical assignments developed by the Plans Section. The Operation Section will have the largest number of personnel. This section is also the section that gets implemented first on any incident. To maintain organization and span of control within the operation section, additional levels of organization can be used as necessary.

- Single Resources
- Strike Teams
- Task Forces
- Groups
- Divisions
- Branches

We will explain each of these in the Resource Management and Span of Control section.

Planning – the planning section is responsible for the collection, evaluation, and display of the incident information, maintaining the status of the resources, and preparing the incident action plan and incident-related documentation. Several of the major functions within planning are maintaining and displaying the Incident Situational Status (**SITSTAT**), maintaining and displaying Resource Status (**RESTAT**), preparing the written Incident Action Plan (**IAP**), preparing the Demobilization Plan, providing investigation and intelligence, providing documentation services, and effectively using technical specialists. Clues and information are processed in the Documentation Unit.

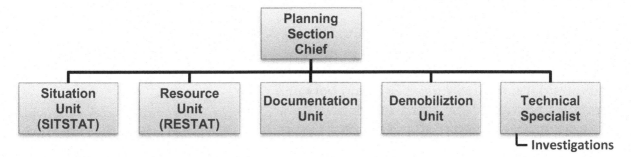

Logistics – the logistics section is responsible for providing adequate services and support to meet all incident and event needs. This will include facilities, equipment, supplies, and personnel. The logistics section can be expanded into two branches – Support Branch and Service Branch.

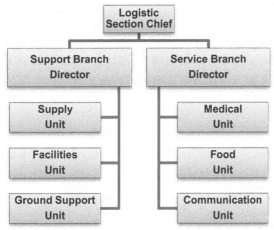

Finance/Administration – the finance/administration section is responsible for keeping track of incident-related costs, personnel, and equipment records and administering procurement contracts associated with the incident or event. They are responsible for the financial activities related to the incident such as procurement, claims, time recording, and cost analysis. This function is normally expanded on larger incidents to handle the on-site financial management. During large complex incidents, it is recommended that the IC delegates this function early.

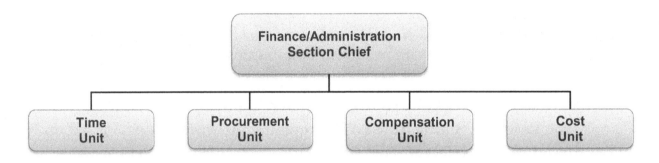

The Command Staff

The Command is also responsible to ensure safety at the incident, create information channels for internal and external stakeholders, and establish liaisons between agencies participating in the incident. The Title of the command staff is Officer.

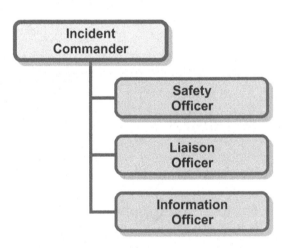

The *Safety Officer* works closely with the Incident Command and Operations Section Chief to ensure the safety of all incident personnel. The Safety Officer can exercise authority to halt any unsafe operations.

The *Liaison Officer* assists the Incident Command by serving as the point of contact for agency representatives that are supporting the effort. In a search, a Family liaison is assigned to communicate with the family. Political Liaison may also be assigned.

The *Information Officer* advises the Incident Command on disseminating information and media relations about the incident. The Information Officer will exchange information and intelligence with the Planning Section. The Incident Command must approve all information that the Information Officer releases. They will coordinate with the media.

The General Staff
The General Staff consists of the four major Section activities of Operations, Planning, Logistics, and Finance/Administration. The title for the sections is Section Chiefs.

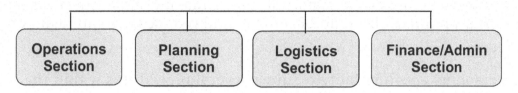

Resource Management and Span of Control

In order to use resources effectively and to ensure that a leader can be effective in their leadership, the use of the span of control is necessary. ICS considers an effective span of control to be a ratio of 1 supervisor/leader to 3-7 subordinates, however, the ratio of 1 to 5 is optimum. If it falls outside of those ranges expansion or consolidation of the organization using resource management techniques may be used to branch out, group together, or divide.

Modular Organization is the use of Branches, Groups, Divisions, and teams as Strike Teams and Task Forces in order to divide and assign functions based on the size and complexity of an incident.

> *Branches* have functional or geographical responsibility for major parts of the incident operations.

> *Groups* divide incident resources into <u>functional</u> areas.

> *Divisions* organize incident resources by <u>geographical</u> areas.

ICS manages resources by organizing them in the following ways:

> <u>**Single Resource**</u> – The smallest unit that can operate independently with common communications and a supervisor is a single resource. An example of a single resource is a K9 and handler.

> <u>**Strike Team**</u> – A combination of the same kind and type of resource with common communications and a leader is a strike team.

> <u>**Task Force**</u> – Any combination of different resources, assembled for a specific task, with common communications and a leader is a task force. An example is an Urban Search and Rescue Task Force due to the various types of resources put together as a team.

During an incident, resources must be managed and accounted for at all times. Resources are people, animals, equipment, materials, or other assets to search and find the missing subject.

The use of taskforces and strike teams allows for maximum effectiveness and use of resources, reduces the span of control, and reduces communications traffic.

Ensuring personnel accountability requires several procedures within the ICS:
- Check-in – this is mandatory for all personnel when arriving at the incident
- Unity of command – ensures everybody has one supervisor.
- Resource status unit – maintains the status of all resources
- Division/Group Assignment Lists – identifies resources with active assignments in the operation section.
- Unit logs – a record of personnel assigned in all organizational elements.

RESTAT (Resource Status) is another way to manage and account for resources is to assign status conditions. Resources assigned to an incident will always be in one of these conditions:

- <u>Available</u> – Resources awaiting an active assignment.

- <u>Assigned</u> – Resource has been assigned and is preparing for or actively engaged in their assignment.

- <u>Out of Service</u> – Resources are on site but not assigned and not available.

Common Terminology
Chain of Command

The Chain of Command refers to a clear and orderly line of authority within the ranks of the incident management organization.

Unity of Command

The Unity of Command means that every person in the organization has a single designated supervisor with whom they report. Do not confuse "Unity of Command" with "Unified Command" Unity of Command means that each person will be given one supervisor and they should not expect to be given information, assignments, or direction from any other than their immediate supervisor.

Incident Facilities: Facilities are established depending on the size and complexity of the incident. The names and functions of incident facilities are standard regardless of the type of incident. The following are common facilities:

Incident Command Post – The location from which the Incident Commander oversees all incident operations and where primary command functions are performed. There is only one ICP for each event and is collocated with the Incident Base.

Staging Areas – Temporary locations where resources are kept while awaiting incident assignment. Most large incidents will have a staging area and some may have several. These are managed by a Staging Area Manager who reports to the Operations Section Chief or Incident Commander if an Operations Section has not been established.

Incident Base – An Incident Base is a location where primary service and support activities are performed. The base is different than staging areas in that resources assigned there are generally out-of-service as compared to those in the staging area that is 'available.'

Helibase – A staffed area where helicopters may land, re-fuel, and be maintained.

Helispot – Helispots are temporary locations where helicopters can land, load, and off-load personnel, equipment, and supplies.

Incident Action Plan

Every incident must have an incident action plan either oral or written. The purpose of the plan is to provide all incident personnel with appropriate direction for future actions. Written plans should be used when it is essential that all levels of a growing organization have a clear understanding of tactical actions associated with their next operational period. A written action plan is required whenever there are two or more jurisdictions involved, the incident will overlap major changes in personnel or go into an additional operational period.

On a simple incident, the use of an ICS 201 better known as an incident debriefing form can be used. A written action plan or Incident Action Plan (IAP) is a combination of additional ICS forms as listed below:

ICS 202 – Incident Objectives

ICS 203 – Organization Assignments

ICS 204 – Assignment Lists

ICS 205 – Communications Plan

ICS 206 – Medical Plan

ICS 207 – Organizational Chart

ICS 208 – Safety Message/Plan

Area Search Map / SITSAT Report

So how does ICS fit into Search & Rescue?

When the first responding resources arrive on the scene, establishing Command will contribute to a successful outcome of finding the subject by identifying objectives and various strategies. Establishing a command structure also contributes to maintaining the safety and accountability of everyone supporting the incident. Searching for missing persons inherently exposes the personnel to a higher risk simply due to personnel going into the woods and possibly covering large geographical areas. The need for accountability forces leadership to know who is where and what tasks are being completed, when they are supposed to return, and what communication frequency they will be on.

Upon arrival on the scene, some of the initial responsibilities of first arriving responders will be to account for personnel using sign-in logs, determine the urgency of the situation, identify where the missing person was last seen or known to have been and gather a physical description of the missing person. Additionally, someone needs to assure that no unnecessary personnel enters and contaminates the likely areas where the subject was known to have been.

While the list of management tasks expands, the Incident Commander still needs to identify these jobs that need to be completed. It is important to establish who the responsible authority is, identify the incident commander, and establish the operations and planning sections early. Operations should quickly identify a staging area for incoming resources.

When responding to the search incident as an initial resource it requires the first arriving authority having jurisdiction personnel to conduct a Size Up of the scene and determine the situation. Evaluate the Operational Risk Management and safety threats to personnel and then implement the ICS Systems using the ICS Forms and delegating functional areas such as Plans and Operations.

ICS Forms

Another characteristic of the standardization of the ICS Features is that the forms are also standardized.

See the appendix for some of the most commonly used forms and the forms that are used to make up the incident action plan (IAP).

ICS Form Name
ICS 201 - Incident Briefing form:
Page 1 - Incident Briefing / Map Sketch
Page 2 - Summary of Current Actions
Page 3 - Current Organization
Page 4 - Resources Summary
ICS 202 - Incident Objectives List
ICS 203 - Organization Assignment List
ICS 204 - Division Assignment List
ICS 205 - Incident Radio Communications Plan
ICS 206 - Medical Plan
ICS 207 - Organizational Chart (requires legal size paper)
ICS 208 - Safety Message/Plan
ICS 209 - Incident Status Summary Report
ICS 210 - Status Change Card
ICS 211 - Incident Check-In Lists
ICS 213 - General Message form
ICS 214 - Unit Log Form
ICS 215 - Operational Planning Worksheet
ICS 215A - Incident Safety Worksheet
ICS 216 - Radio Requirements Worksheet
ICS 217 - Radio Frequency Assignment Worksheet
ICS 218 - Support Vehicle Inventory form
ICS 219 - Resource Status Card
ICS219-2 - Crew (green)
ICS219-4 - Helicopter (blue)
ICS219-6 - Aircraft (orange)
ICS219-7 - Dozer (yellow)
ICS 220 - Air Operations Summary
ICS 221 - Demobilization Checkout and Instructions

References:

Boy Scouts of America – Merit Badge Series – Search and Rescue – 2018
Charlotte, NC

The 9/11 Commission Report

National Incident Management System – http://www.fema.gov/national-incident-management-system
Washington DC December 2008

National Response Framework – 3rd Edition – 2016 Washington DC

National Wildfire Coordinating Group – NFES 2441 – October 1994 principles and features of ICS, module 2 I 200

National wildfire coordinating group – NFES 24155 - October 1994 history of ICS

Chapter 4   Introduction to Basic Land Navigation

- Importance of Orienting
- Different Types of Maps
- Georeferencing Coordinates and reading and using a grid reader
- Measuring Distance by Pace
- Compass
- Map Exercise(s)

Upon completion of this chapter and the related course activities, the student will be able to meet the following objectives ASTM F3098 (16) 8.1 – 8.4:

1. Describe the various methods used to navigate
2. Describe the various types of maps used in search and rescue and the associated features
3. Know the differences between topographical and road maps and the advantages and disadvantages of each.
4. Demonstrate the understanding of the two types of geo-referencing systems
   a. Latitude and Longitude
   b. United States National Grid
5. Demonstrate measuring distance by pace count
6. Describe why the map datum is important and how it relates to maps
7. Describe the basic features of an orienteering compass
8. Demonstrate the "waist-high" and "eye-level" techniques used to determine a bearing

Handouts:
- USGS Topographical map of Local Area to scale with USNG Grid system
- Map Symbols – E.1
- Stride Sheet – H.1

Exercises:
- Pace count of 100 meters
- Orienting without a compass
- Compass Uses – Box and Triangle 360 degree

Props for Class:
- Full-size USGS 7.5 Minute Quadrangle Map
- World Globe

Importance of Being Geographically Oriented

Most people have a basic sense of direction when it comes down to their geographical location. At some point in time we all find ourselves asking questions like: Where am I? Where am I going? How long will it take for me to get there? How do I get back? When we are driving somewhere these questions may be raised but we have the advantage of identifiable landmarks and street signs to assist us. When we enter the wilderness environment, we certainly lose most, if not all, of the navigation aids that we take for granted in our routine life. During and after a disaster, common landmarks and street signs that normally assist us can be destroyed, displaced, or non-existent as shown in the picture below on the right.

Most trails have markings for recreational hikers to follow. However, the problem arises for search and rescue personnel because they usually have to operate in areas without markings. In survival training, there are several tricks of the trade. An example is an old adage that moss only grows on the north side of the tree. It does have merit depending upon where the tree is located in relation to the majority of sunlight. For example, in the middle latitudes of the northern hemisphere, the south sides of trees usually receive sunlight during the year which means that moss will not grow in sunny areas. This information is certainly useful and in a survival situation may make the difference between life and death. Knowing these skills does not ensure anyone's survival. Basic outdoor skills will increase your skills

and confidence in the outdoors whether you are a hiker, hunter, ride mountain bikes, an adventure guide, or someone who would like to get involved with search and rescue. Each outdoor enthusiast should know how to read a map, how to orient the map to the local terrain, how to use a compass not only to follow a direction of travel, but also help to find your location, and understand how to measure distances both on a map and in the terrain. These outdoor skills are easily learned, fun to practice, and could one day help you during a survival situation.

We can use several different methods to navigate or to help us find out where we are:

- **Celestial navigation** – observing the sun, moon, stars, and planets (This can be difficult to use when fog and clouds appear, obscuring visibility of the planets, sun, and stars)
- **Pilotage** – using visible natural and manmade features such as sea marks and beacons
- **Dead reckoning** – using course and speed to determine the position
- **Off-course navigation** – allows for variables in heading by deliberately aiming to the one side of the destination. (Also referred to as "aiming off" or "off-set aiming")
- **Electronic navigation** – using electronic equipment such as radio navigation and satellite navigation system (GPS) to follow a course to a location

Maps – Tools for Navigation

A map is a graphical representation of the Earth's surface drawn to scale and reproduced on a flat piece of paper.

There are a variety of maps and charts, however, maps used for search and rescue should adequately reflect the terrain within the search area. The map also needs to have the appropriate amount of detail of the area for those traveling on foot. For a wilderness search, the use of a topographical map is most appropriate; for an urban search a planimetric map may be the most appropriate; an aerial search for a missing plane, an aeronautical chart/map would be the most appropriate; and for a water search of a bay, river, or lake, a nautical chart/map would be the most appropriate. Generally, a topographic map is the map of choice for search and rescue.

As a minimum, maps for land navigation should provide the following data:

- An accurate depiction of terrain on a scale that is realistic for resources
- The major terrain features such as hills, valleys, and ridges
- "Man-made" features such as buildings, trails, and roads
- An accurate depiction of measurable relief, elevation, and contour (lay of the land)
- A georeferencing coordinate system (Latitude/Longitude, UTM, and/or USNG)
- The location of water and watercourses

Maps are an essential part of any search activity. There are various types of maps, all of which may be valuable at the search incident. The types of maps used include:

- Planimetric Maps
- Orthophoto Maps
- US Topo Maps
- Topographic Maps

Maps are the best tool available the various items on the Earth's surface from contours, water features, buildings, roads, and vegetation.

Planimetric Maps *(Street Map)* are two-dimensional maps and are the most common type of map used by most people. These are basic street maps. They illustrate horizon positions on the map but not any vertical information. Planimetric maps illustrate roads, buildings, parks, lakes, and rivers and are usually labeled. Most people are accustomed to these types of maps simply because of their availability and usefulness in everyday activities. The better-drawn maps are scaled, where a given distance anywhere on the map represents the distance in the field. They also indicate North and have a key to identify the symbols used on the map. These maps are usually drawn to a scale that provides a reasonable trade-off of coverage with detail for navigating by automobile. The maps are useful for search and rescue operations in the urban environment.

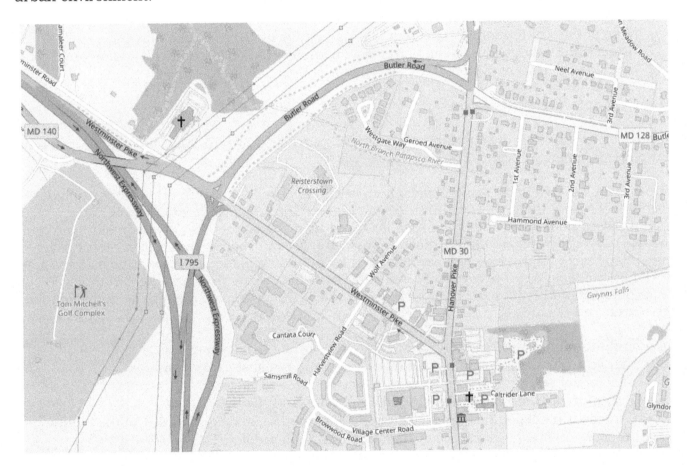

Orthophoto Maps (Aerial Photo Map) illustrate features of the land by using color-enhanced photographic images that have been processed to show detail in their true position. They may include elevation changes and some man-made feature labeling. The National Agriculture Imagery Program (NAIP) acquires aerial imagery during the agricultural growing seasons in the continental U.S. A primary goal of the NAIP program is to make digital ortho photography available to governmental agencies and the public within a year of acquisition. They are very detailed and can be down to 1 meter. The orthophotos can be found at http://datagateway.nrcs.usda.gov.

Orthophoto Maps (Aerial Photo Map)

The newest maps – combining the traditional USGS 7.5 Quadrangle with Orthoimage. These maps can be found online of The National Maps http://nationalmap.gov/.

In 1992 the 7.5 min. map series was completed and recently has been replaced by the National Map providing public access to geospatial data. US topo is the new generation of digital topographical maps and is available free on the web and is constructed in portable document file (PDF) format with geospatial extension (GEOPDF) format. These can be found in the National Map.

Topographic Maps portray the shape and elevation of the terrain while showing a graphic representation of selected man-made and natural features plotted to scale. These maps are generally used in search incidents because of the detailed information it affords both the search management and field resources.

The topographical maps portray both natural and man-made features. They show and name works of nature including mountains, valleys, plains, lakes, rivers, and vegetation. The maps also identify the principal work of men such as roads, boundaries, transmission lines, trails, and major buildings.

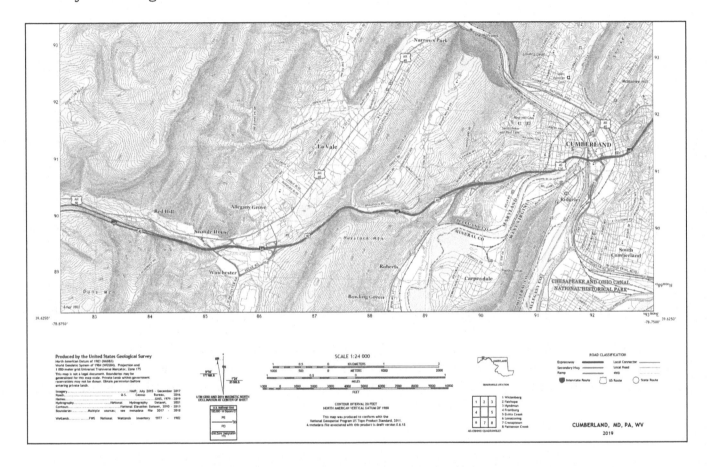

Today United States Geological Survey (USGS) has digitized data and this is based on the existing topographical maps. These maps can be found online of The National Maps http://nationalmap.gov/.

The best-known USGS maps are the 1:24,000 scale topographical map, also known as 7.5-minute quadrangles, which are produced by the United States Geologic Service (USGS).

What makes up a map? The 10 items map up a map: 1) Data Frame, 2) Legend, 3) Title, 4) North Arrows, 5) Scale and scale bar, 6) Citation, 7) Grid Coordinates, 8) Map Orientation, 9) Map Datum, and 10) Insert Map.

Scale:

The USGS produces 7.5 minute, 1:24,000 scale topographic maps. The map covers an area of 7.5 minutes of latitude and longitude distance at a 1:24,000 scale. A scale of 1:24,000 indicates that one inch on the map represents 24,000 inches or 2,000 feet on the ground or within the area depicted on the map. A scale of 1:24,000 is the best map to use for search and rescue work since it provides the terrain detail needed by field searchers to identify area terrain features that should help keep them oriented during their search of the area. Orthographic maps may have a scale of 1:12,000.

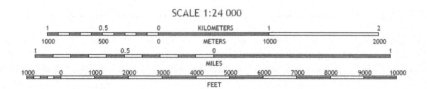

All Topographical Maps are oriented to True North. There are three different Norths on the map. There is True North, Magnetic North, and Grid North.

True North is the direction of lines of longitude which converge on the North Pole.

Grid North is the grid lines of a map projection. An example of a grid projection is the USNG covered earlier in this chapter.

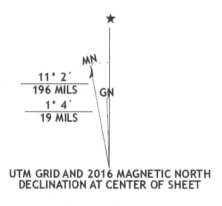

UTM GRID AND 2016 MAGNETIC NORTH DECLINATION AT CENTER OF SHEET

Magnetic North is a point on the earth's surface where the planet's magnetic field points directly downwards. The magnetic North pole moves over time due to changes in the earth's core. Magnetic North is near, but distinct from True North.

Magnetic declination is the angle between the magnetic north (the direction the north end of a compass needle points) and True North. Magnetic declination varies from place to place and changes with the passage of time. It is important to find out what the magnetic declination is for the search area. When communicating your bearing it is important to indicate what north you are using, True or Magnetic North.

Contour Lines:

One uniqueness of a topographical map is that it has a contour line representing elevation above sea level representing the Earth's features accurately and to scale on a two-dimensional surface. The **brown lines** on the map are referred to as Contour Lines and represent areas of equal elevation. The distance between the Contour Lines can indicate a rise or fall in elevation in increments of feet or meters, as explained in the legend at the bottom of the map.

CONTOUR INTERVAL 20 FEET
NORTH AMERICAN VERTICAL DATUM OF 1988

Generally, the closer the lines are together, the steeper the terrain; The Contour Lines that are farther apart represent flatter terrain. Contour intervals can be 20, 40, or 80 feet. The contour interval will be in the legend at the bottom of the map.

There are several types of contour lines; two of them are index and intermediate. An index contour line will indicate the elevation numerically on the line in feet above mean sea level (MSL) if there is enough space along the line to place the number and is every fifth line with four intermediate lines in between every two index lines.

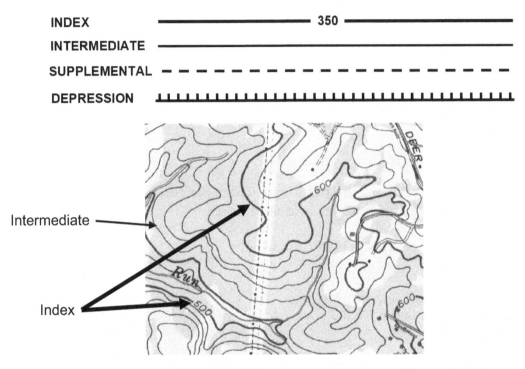

Contour lines will form several **Contour Features**:

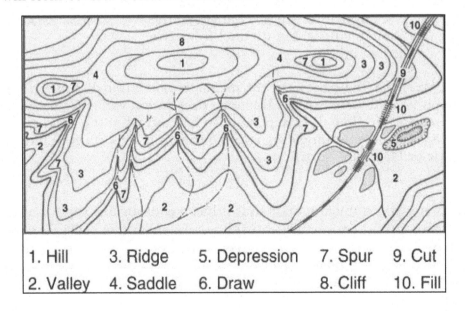

1. Hill	3. Ridge	5. Depression	7. Spur	9. Cut
2. Valley	4. Saddle	6. Draw	8. Cliff	10. Fill

It is essential to identify features of a topographical map such as a valley, hill, saddle, depression, ridge, drainage, and cliff. These features can assist you in identifying your location.

Because so much information is contained on a standard USGS topographic map, a common symbol set is used. Unfortunately, because the symbol set is so expansive, only a few of the symbols are shown in the legend's lower right collar or border area. A complete set of symbol legends can be viewed and/or purchased from the USGS at https://pubs.usgs.gov/gip/TopographicMapSymbols/topomapsymbols.pdf/

Topographic maps will have a legend for basic symbols for Road Classifications. Generally, man-made permanent objects like buildings, railroad tracks, telephone lines, and roads are shown in **Black**. Individual houses may be shown as small black squares. For larger buildings, the actual shapes are mapped. Elevation markers (are black) ▲^{980}. Water features such as lakes, rivers, and streams are shown in **Blue**. Contour lines and some other "earth features" are drawn in **Brown**. Areas of denser vegetation are shown in **Green** and less dense areas and cultivated or cleared areas are shown in **White**. At one time, purple was used as a revision color to show all feature changes. Currently, **Purple** is not used in the current map system, but the purple features are still present on many existing maps. **Red** is used for land grids and important roads. Some roads and trails, railroads, boundaries, and other cultural features will also be **black**.

Topographical maps are the most used and primary maps in search and rescue.

Grids are outlined on the border of the topographical map and will have tic marks and numbers indicating the grid reference numbers. On a topographical map are the Grids for Latitude/Longitude and US National Grid/UTM.

Map Datum - a datum is the mathematical model of the Earth we use to calculate the coordinates on any map, chart, or survey system. All coordinates reference some particular set of numbers for the size and shape of the Earth. A geodetic datum or geodetic system is a coordinate system, and a set of reference points, used for locating places on the Earth. There are both horizontal and vertical datums. Most topographical maps use North America Datum or NAD. There are two with older topographical maps having NAD27 completed in 1927 or NAD83 completed in 1983. Both of these are horizontal datums and can be off by several to 10s of meters. WGS 84 is the World Geodetic System of 1984 used by the Department of Defense and defined by the National Geospatial-Intelligence Agency (NGA). NAD83 and WGS84 are equivalent.

On the lower-left corner of a topographic map, there is a note that will describe the Map Datum.

Produced by the United States Geological Survey
North American Datum of 1983 (NAD83)
World Geodetic System of 1984 (WGS84). Projection and
1 000-meter grid:Universal Transverse Mercator, Zone 17S

Mapped, edited, and published by the Geological Survey

Control by USGS and NOS/NOAA

Topography by photogrammetric methods from aerial photographs taken 1947. Field checked 1949

Polyconic projection. 10,000-foot grid ticks based on Maryland coordinate system,
Pennsylvania coordinate system, south zone, and West Virginia coordinate system, north zone
1000-meter Universal Transverse Mercator grid ticks, zone 17, shown in blue. 1927 North American Datum
To place on the predicted North American Datum 1983 move the projection lines 6 meters south and
22 meters west as shown by dashed corner ticks

What is geo-referencing?

Georeferencing means associating items such as maps, images, and places with locations in physical space. It is how to position data can be related to a ground system of geographic coordinates.

A map datum is a coordinate system, and a set of reference points used to locate places on earth. Since there is a multitude of datums, everyone must be using the same map datum during SAR incidents. If you're not using the same datum a location provided by one SAR provider may be interpreted by another as a different location. Within the United States and the search and rescue community, it has been determined that the North American Datum 1983 (NAD 83) and World Geodetic System 1984 (WGS 84) shall be used. The difference between these two map datums scaled at 1:24000 or smaller is Insignificant and shall be considered as equivalent.

Two geo-referencing methods are typically used for search and rescue operations within the United States. These are known as point reference systems. The two-point reference systems are the United States National Grid (US NG) and the geographical coordinate system, better known as latitude and longitude.

Geo-Reference System	United States National Grid (USNG)	Latitude/Longitude DD-MM.mm
Land/Wilderness SAR Responder	Primary	Secondary
Aeronautical SAR Responder	Secondary	Primary

Coordinate Grid Systems

Unfortunately for mapmakers, the earth is a sphere and this makes it difficult to represent the map accurately on a flat surface. For example, if you were on a large lake, standing in a boat, the horizon would be about three miles away. Objects farther away would begin to "disappear" or go below the horizon because of the curvature of the earth.

There are two coordinate grid systems used in SAR.
Latitude and Longitude, when combined, specify the position of any location on the surface of the earth without consideration of altitude or depth.

United States National Grid (USNG) which is equivalent to the Military Grid Reference System (MGRS) is based on Universal Transverse Mercator (UTM) and uses a Cartesian grid laid out to locate positions on the surface of the earth. This grid is not a single map projection but a series of sixty grids divided by 6-degree bands of longitude.

Latitude/ Longitude

The world is round, better known as a globe, which begins nowhere and ends nowhere. However, there are two major points which are the North and South Poles. Halfway between these two poles is the equator which splits the globe in half with the northern half considered the Northern Hemisphere and the southern half considered the Southern Hemisphere. The Equator is at an equal distance from both the North and South Poles; hence the name, Equator.

From the North or South Pole to the Equator is 10,000 kilometers. The distance to the center of the Earth is 6,371 kilometers. The earth is round with the equator, lines of latitude and longitude are a circle around the earth. Measuring from the equator or the prime meridian requires one to understand the **arc angle of a circle** or arc measurement which is in *degrees*. The measurement is from the core of the earth out to the equator with the other line to your location North or South of the equator for Latitude and East or West of the prime meridian for Longitude.

Latitude

Lines of latitude are parallel to the equator thus they never intersect and are also known as **Parallels.** Latitude is measured in degrees North and South of the equator from the core of the earth. The Equator is located at zero (0) degrees of latitude and the poles are located at 90 degrees. Lines of Latitude are read and written first, they are displayed on the right and left sides of a map.

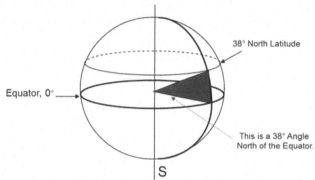

The illustration shows a line of latitude 38° North of the equator from the center of the earth.

Longitude

Lines of longitude go from North to the South Pole as semi-circles and are at right angles to lines of latitude. Lines of Longitude are also known as Meridians. The Prime Meridian is zero (0) degrees of longitude. The Prime Meridian runs through the Royal Observatory Greenwich, England. Degrees of longitude are measured from 0 to 180 degrees to the East and West of the Prime Meridian. Lines of Longitude are read and written last, they are displayed on the top and bottom of a map.

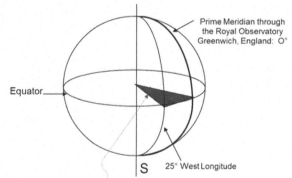

This is a 25 ° Angle West of the Prime Meridian

The illustration shows a line of longitude 25° west of the Prime Meridian from the center of the earth.

Latitude and Longitude on a Topo Map

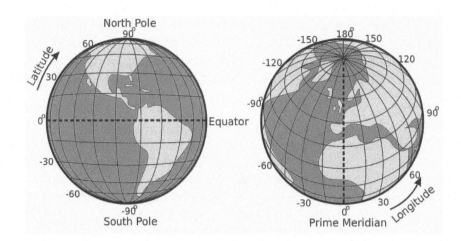

Latitude and Longitude is a geographical coordinate system in which coordinates are expressed in angular measurements. lines of longitude are divided into 360 degrees, each degree is broken down into 60 minutes, and each minute in tenths of a minute. It is used by pilots and boaters due to the longer distances that they travel.

Latitude and Longitude should be documented and read in the following format, Degrees, Minutes, and Decimal Minutes (DDD° MM.mmm). Latitude is always read and written first followed by Longitude. For example, the coordinates of the US capital are N 38° 53.383' W 77° 00.547'

When communicating Latitude and Longitude coordinates, it is important to convey them correctly. The latitude and longitude coordinates above should be read as: *"North Three eight degrees, five three decimal three eight three minutes by West seven seven degrees, zero zero decimal five four seven degrees"*. The words, "degrees," "minutes," and "decimal" must be spoken.

> ° = Degrees ' = Minutes " = Seconds . = Decimal

It is important to understand Latitude and Longitude when working with air assets. It is especially important when coordinating ground assets with a search and rescue helicopter or plane.

U.S. National Grid System (USNG)

The Department of Homeland Security (DHS) and the United States Search and Rescue Committee recommends the use of a nationally defined coordinate system for all spatial referencing, mapping, and reporting. The United States National Grid (USNG) is a multi-purpose location system of grid references used in the United States. It provides a nationally consistent "language of location", optimized for local applications, in a compact, user-friendly format. The USNG was adopted as a national standard by the Federal Geographic Data Committee (FGDC) of the US Government in 2001. USNG relies on the Universal Transverse Mercator (UTM) coordinate system and is applied not only in the United States but also worldwide.

The goal of the USNG is to provide a uniform, nationally-consistent rectangular grid system that is interoperable across maps at different scales, as well as with GPS and other location-based systems. It is intended to provide a frame of reference for describing and communicating locations that are easier to use than latitude/longitude. It is easy to learn, teach, and use. USNG can be extended for use worldwide as a universal grid reference system and can be easily plotted on USGS topographic maps by using a simple "read right, then up" method. So when reading USNG read from the Left to the Right first then Bottom to Top second as a simple **"Read Right, Then Up"**.

The coordinates are easily translated to distance, as they are actually in meters. Thus the distance between two coordinates can quickly be determined in the field.

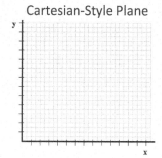

Locating points on large-scale maps and for ground navigation is best accomplished using a Cartesian-style plane coordinate. USNG coordinates define two-dimensional, horizontal positions similar to the Cartesian-style plane while maintaining the projection of the earth's curved surface.

The USNG is an alpha-numeric reference system that overlays the UTM coordinate system.

As stated earlier, USNG is not a single map projection but a series of sixty grids divided by 6-degree bands of longitude extending from 84 degrees north latitude to 80 degrees south latitude.

The zones are numbered 1 through 60 west to east, beginning at 180 degrees west longitude.

Latitude zone characters are letters that designate eight degree incremental zones extending north and south from the equator. Beginning at 80° south and proceeding northward, 20 bands are lettered C through X, omitting I and O. These bands are all 8° increments except for band X which is a 12° band (between 72–84 N).

A USGN coordinate 10S GJ 0683 4468.

In the above coordinate 10 is the 6° Longitude Band, S is the 8° Latitude band, so 18S is known as the Grid Zone Designator. The GJ is the 100,000 meter Square Identifier. The 0683 4468 is the Grid Coordinate which is read right then up. The eight digits Grid Coordinates will provide 10-meter accuracy which is the standard for search and rescue. To obtain 1-meter accuracy the use of a Global Positioning System (GPS) unit would be needed.

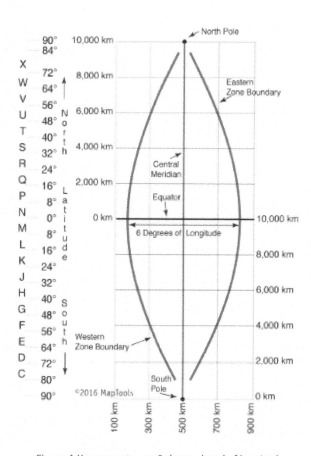

Figure 4-X represents one 6-degree band of longitude

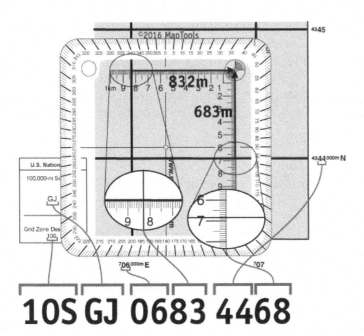

Figure 4-X represents a grid tool on a map

USNG can plot points down to 1 meter. Various maps are gridded in 1-kilometer quadrants, and each kilometer can be broken down to tenths or hundredths. Blue tick marks along the edge of the topographic quadrangle maps are the UTM reference points at one kilometer increments.

Doing a search and rescue operation the Grid Zone Designator and the 100,000 meter Square Identifier is normally dropped off, only the eight-digit Grid Coordinate is used. Some State agencies have developed a map with the USNG Zone Designator and the 100,000 meter Square Identifier.
See Example below

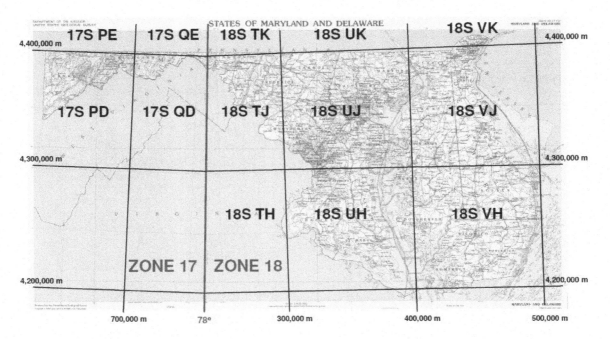

Figure 4-X United States national grid of the state of Maryland

Plotting USNG Points on a Map

When working with USNG coordinates it is beneficial to use a grid reader. There are many types of grid readers and they all work differently. A grid reader is usually printed on a transparent plastic sheet. When using a grid reader to plot points on a map, the scale on the grid reader must match the scale of the map.

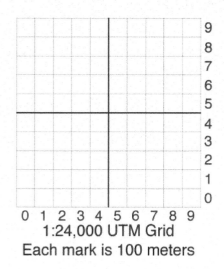

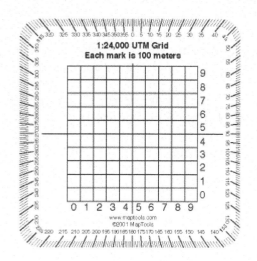

The two grid readers above are laid directly over the 1-kilometer grid on the map to be able to determine the hundredths and tenths of a kilometer.

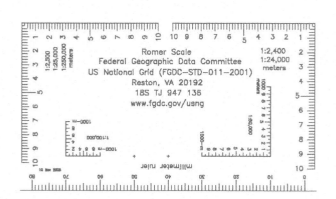

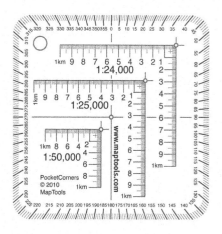

The two grid readers above are used by starting at the kilometer intersecting X, Y coordinate and is slide to the right then up to the location to obtain the hundredths and tenth of a kilometer.

Some grid readers have a compass rose built in to assist in plotting bearings (azimuths) on a map. There are many online resources on how to locate coordinates using grid reader and USNG.

Measuring Distance by Pace

Keeping track of your distance traveled is essential in search and rescue. To find where you are, using a map, you can find prominent landmarks and features that can be distinguished both in the field and on your map. Or, you can locate your starting point on the map and follow a known heading and approximate distance and use that data to calculate your location on the map. Location plotting is also beneficial at a search incident to identify and document where a clue is located. The second method is preferred since it does not rely on terrain features.

The distance can be estimated by knowing the length of one's pace, stride (a person's double step) and multiplying it by the number of paces/strides taken.

The English term "mile" is derived from a Roman term that means "1,000 Roman Paces" or double steps. The Romans considered the pace to be five times the length of a Roman legionnaire's foot and, thus, the Roman mile was 5,000 feet. It wasn't until much later that the English mile was redefined as 5,280 feet.

One step is the distance one walks when measuring from one foot to the other. A pace or stride, on the other hand, is equivalent to every two steps, or the distance between where one foot strikes the ground and where the same foot strikes the ground again.

Measuring your pace or stride is sometimes referred to as finding your "tally". To find your tally, you will need to set up a course in your local terrain and practice. Use a long piece of string and measuring tape to set up a meandering route in the woods of some easily remembered distance such as 100 meters or 100 feet. It is important not to use a straight-line course because your stride will need to naturally adjust for low branches, thick underbrush, and other natural obstacles. Walk the round-trip string route several times over several days both ways and keep track of the number of strides it takes to cover the course. Walk the route with your pack in the morning while you are still energetic, and then also walk the route with your pack in the late afternoon after several hours of hiking or other physical exercises. Once you have completed the course several times, under several conditions, take the number of paces/strides for each trial and obtain an average. (Add up the total paces/strides and divide the sum by the numbers of trials.) This will be your personal "tally" for determining distances in your terrain. For example, if your course was 100 feet long and it took an average of 20 paces/strides to cover the course, your tally is 20 strides for 100 feet or five feet per pace/stride.

Keep in mind that paces/strides can vary substantially from one individual to another, so individuals need to know their pace/stride length.

Example of planning out a route – A search team member has a pace count of 60 paces for 100 meters. If they have to travel 850 meters how many paces would the search team member have?

60 paces x (850/100) = 510. When traversing overland look for catching features and measure each point.

Pace Beads, Ranger Beads, Tally Beads

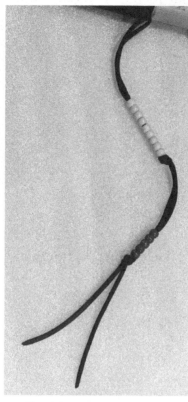

Figure 4x Pace Counting Beads

Military, SAR, and some recreational hikers use "Tally Beads" or "Pace Beads" which are beads on a string for each "Tally Step Index" (total number of Tally Steps for a known distance). Some may use an inventory type clicker.

There are two methods to construct tally beads:
- Metric-based
- English-based

Metric Based Pacing Beads (Most-used system)
Four beads are located above the knot and nine beads are located below the knot. The four top beads each represent 1000 meters or 1 kilometer. The nine bottom beads each represent 100 meters. Each time that you reach your Tally Step Index you pull down or pull up one of the bottom beads to represent 100 meters. After performing this process nine times (900 meters) the next time that you reach your tally step-index you would pull up or pull down one of the top beads to represent 1,000 meters or one kilometer. Then start the process over again.

- Upper beads (kilometer) counter: four 1,000-meter (one kilometer) beads
- Lower beads: nine 100-meter (1/10 kilometer) beads

English-based Pacing Beads
The English system works on the statute mile instead of kilometers. The method of use is identical to the method stated above with the Metric Based Pacing Beads; the only difference is measurement kilometer versus mile.

- Upper half-mile counter: six 880-yard (or 1/2 mile) beads
- Lower march counter: seven 110-yard (or 1/16 mile) beads

Compass:

Today's modern compass is a great deal more precise and offers, to a large extent, more added features such as phosphorescent parts that can be seen in the dark, rotating bezel, orienting lines, mirror, etc.

Even though there are numerous types of compasses developed for specific needs, for the purpose of this course we will focus on the orienteering type compass.

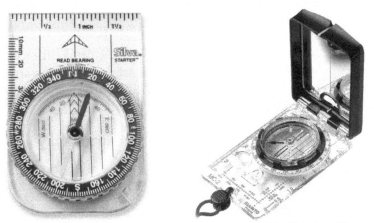

Figure 4x Basic Orienteering Compass & one with Sighting Mirror

Orienteering compasses are the ideal choice in search and rescue because of the additional features that allow for easier use than other types of compasses.

An orienteering compass includes the following basic parts:

- Scales
- Base Plate
- Direction of Travel Arrow
- Magnifier
- Index Pointer

- Rotating Dial or Bezel
- Declination Marks
- Orienting Arrow

- Magnetic Needle

Below are the various features of an orienteering compass.

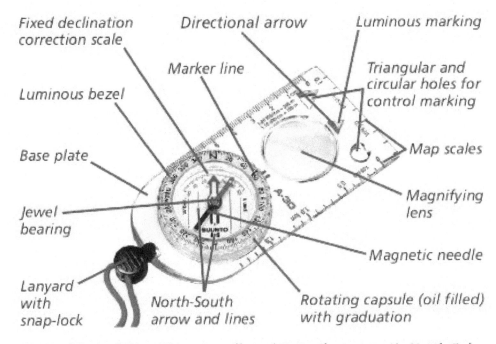

The red end of the compass needle points to the magnetic North Pole.

Orienteering style compasses used for search and rescue usually have a clear base plate, a fluid-filled housing encompassing the magnetic needle with 2° increments on the rotating dial, and a sighting mirror.

The base plate is usually clear but can be yellow or black. It is rectangular with edge measurement markings and scales.

The rotating dial, also called the bezel, (as shown) is marked clockwise in 360 degrees. For required field accuracy, the dial must be in 2-degree increments. The orienting lines on the bottom of the capsule inside the rotating bezel are used with a map to obtain navigational headings. Most compasses also have an outline of a compass arrow (also within the dial) or possibly two marks near the north end of the capsule. These items are used to align the magnetic needle with the orienting arrow so that a bearing can be followed in the outdoor setting. This has informally been called the "box" or "dog house."

The magnetic needle for most compasses has the red or night-visible ends of the needle pointing towards magnetic north. In high-quality compasses, the magnetic needle usually pivots on a jeweled bearing for smooth action. To help the needle move smoothly and settle quickly, the dial is filled with a non-freezing liquid to reduce shakiness.

The **Direction of Travel Arrow** is a line inscribed in the base plate of the compass, the base of which forms the index line (or, if you are on a ship, referred to as a "lubber line"). It is important to note that the ***direction of travel arrow should always be pointing in the desired direction of travel*** while navigating.

The index line is located where the degree reading (also referred to as an azimuth) is read, usually at the bottom of the direction-of-travel arrow. The index line can also be referred to as the "index mark."

The sighting mirror is usually on a hinged cover of the compass, which has a fine line that runs from top to bottom at the center of the mirror. This centerline is an extension of the direction-of-travel arrow and allows the compass to be used more accurately at eye level.

Before we start talking about using the compass, let's discuss headings. Most of us focus on North, South, East, and West, which we refer to as the cardinal points or directions. A compass rose (see Fig. 4x) is graduated in 360 degrees and the cardinal points are separated by 90 degrees starting at 0 degrees being north, 90 degrees is east, 180 degrees is south, 270 degrees is west, and we find ourselves back at 360 or 0 degrees again at North. North can also be referred to as 360 degrees.

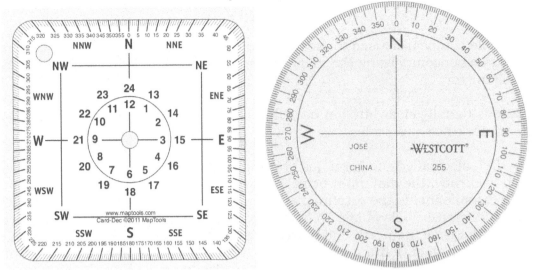

Figure 4x Compass Rose

We can add cardinal points by using North East (NE) being 45°, South East (SE) 135°, South West (SW) 225°, and North West (NW) 315°. However, it is preferable to provide only the numerical value of the degree heading to achieve your desired direction.

Determining a Bearing for an Object in the Field

There are two methods to determine a navigational bearing: the "waist-high" and the "eye-level". The method used is based on the type of compass being used, either with or without a sighting mirror.

Waist-High Method:

Determining a bearing of an object:

1. Hold the compass in front of you between waist-high and chest-high. Be sure to keep the compass level and not tilted, this will keep the needle from contacting the top of the capsule and affecting the heading. It is also important to stand straight and in line with your direction of travel, elbows close to your body. This position assures that as you turn your body and compass toward the object that you will be in line with the object and on a correct compass heading.

2. Holding the compass level, with one hand, rotate the bezel until the "N" on the bezel is aligned with the red end of the magnetic needle. Note that the "orienteering lines" are indeed parallel with the magnetic needle.

3. Move the compass from the chest-high position to read the bearing to the object. The bearing to the object is the number of degrees on the bezel that is aligned with the index line, which is an extension of the direction of travel arrow.

4. Note: any ferrous metal near the compass needle will distort the reading. Since the magnetic needle is attached to ferrous metal it is important to keep it away from metal objects.

Eye Level Method:
Bring the compass up to your eye. Position it so that you can see the object in the notch at the top of the mirror. While keeping the bezel level, rotate the bezel until the North- pointing needle is boxed or inside the outline on the capsule. Align the vertical index line and object all in the same line. Fine-tune the bezel to keep the needle boxed. Read the degree at the intersection of the bezel and index line.

Understanding forward and back bearings
There are two types of bearings, Forward and Back.

The forward bearing is from your current location to a point or object in the distance.

For example, from where you are standing, you may want to get the bearing to a tower in the distance. Using one of the two methods above (The waist or eye method) align the direction of travel arrow to your target. Rotate the bezel until the magnetic arrow is "in the dog house". You may now read the bearing to the object (number of degrees) on the bezel that is aligned with the index line. This would be your forward bearing to the tower.

Another example of a forward bearing is with a known azimuth from your current location. Set the desired degree on the bezel at the index line. Holding the compass level, rotate your body and the compass as one until you box the needle. Find an object in the field that lines up with the index line and use it as a landmark/steering point.

Back Azimuth - A back azimuth is a projection of the azimuth from the origin to the opposite side of the azimuth circle. There are 360 degrees in the azimuth circle, so the opposite direction would be 180 degrees (half of 360 degrees) from the azimuth.

A back azimuth is calculated by adding 180° to the azimuth when the azimuth is less than 180°, or by subtracting 180° from the azimuth if it is more than 180°. For example, if an azimuth is 320°, the back azimuth would be 320° - 180° = 140°. If the azimuth is 30°, the back azimuth would be 180° + 30° = 210°.

Chapter 5 – The Missing Subject and Their Behavior

Objectives:
- The student shall understand the importance of a lost or missing person questionnaire. *ASTM F3098 (16) - 12.2*
- The student shall be able to demonstrate how to conduct an interview with a reporting party to obtain information for the lost person questionnaire and understand planning and searching data.
- The student shall demonstrate based on the information collected about the lost or missing person be able to complete and explain the use of a search urgency chart. *ASTM F3098 (16) - 12.1*
- The student shall have a basic understanding of the concept of what is lost person behavior is and understand the subject categories of lost person behavior.
- The Student shall be able to define: *ASTM F3098 (16) - 12.3*
    - Last Known Point (LKP)
    - Point Last Seen (PLS)
    - Initial Planning Point (IPP)
- The student shall understand the influences and factors that may affect a person's behavior based on health, mentality, past experience, and the environment in which there lost within.

Initial Response – First Notice

When a person is believed to be missing or lost it may be minutes, hours, if not days before someone notices that they are absent, lost, or missing. This is known as **First Notice**. If it's a child, a parent within minutes will notice that their child is missing. But for an adult, it could be hours if not days before someone notices that they have not heard from or seen them. It is critical to ascertain the time and date that they were last seen. Depending on the age of the missing person the sense of urgency can be high especially if it's a missing kid under the age of six or an adult with dementia or mental issues that could affect their overall well-being (suicidal) of the missing person.

No matter what the situation is it should always be considered an emergency, and someone must report it to the proper authorities. The person reporting it to the proper authorities is typically known as the ***reporting party*** and the missing or lost person is called the ***subject*** of the search. We must establish who we are looking for. An immediate response is essential until first responders arrive and determine the accuracy of the information and the urgency of the situation.

No matter what your role is it is critical to gather as much information as possible if the reporting party comes to you. Your role may be a park ranger, a law enforcement officer, 911 dispatcher, first responder, or an incident commander. This is typically known as the First Notice.

The first initial action once a **Reporting Party** has contacted you is to conduct a basic interview of the reporting party, complete the lost person questionnaire with the focus on planning and searching data, determine search urgency, conduct a proximity search of the immediate area and establish a sign-in sheet.

Obtain necessary information of the reporting party such as their name, contact information such as a phone number, and how to reconnect with them.

Get all the necessary information to determine:
- if this is truly a problem?
- where did the person go missing from?
- who last saw the missing person and how were they?
- how long have they been missing?
- how did this situation occur?
- how serious is it or could get?
- what is the relation between the reporting party and the subject?

In addition to the Reporting Party, you should inquire others in the area if they witnessed anything unusual or could shed any information on the situation. Make sure to get the witness's contact information and document what they heard, saw, or witnessed.

Interviewing Witnesses, Reporting Party, and Other Sources:

Remember the basis of the Five W's – Who, What, When, Where, and Why are questions whose answers help in information gathering or problem-solving such as finding a missing person. The sixth question is How?

What Happened? – Overdue, heard shot fired, the group split up and someone did not return

Where? – At the trailhead, house, at the car, what is the environment like – Urban, Rural, Wilderness, hilly, seen last where, what direction did they go.

When? – date/time last seen, the time they were supposed to return/show up, review itinerary.

Who? – name and description of the missing person and wearing what

Why? – why did they go missing – mental/physical – family, overcommitted.

Lost Person Questionnaire

There are several forms including a blank note pad that can be used to assist you in conducting the interview with the reporting party. The most common form is the Lost Person Questionnaire. See appendix. It is highly recommended that due to the potential criminal nature of a lost or missing person that the interview be conducted by law enforcement. They are trained as investigators and interviewers to ensure an effective interview is conducted. Until law enforcement shows up gathering basic information from the reporting party can assist with initial actions which could produce the location of the missing subject. Always remember that the collection of this data is an interview, not an interrogation. Leave the investigation up to law enforcement.

Questions should be asked calmly and keeping them focused on providing basic information:
1. name and address of the subject
2. age of the subject
3. sex of the subject
4. race of the subject
5. the height and weight of the subject
6. type, style, and color of clothing subject was last wearing
7. the location of the Point Last Seen (PLS) or Last Known Position (LKP)
8. experience/ability
9. the activity being conducted before going missing
10. missing how long
11. physical/mental/emotional state of the subject
12. missing from where

Based on this initial interview will assist in establishing a **well-researched Subject Profile**. This well-researched subject profile may provide you with the behavior of your missing/lost person in the past, current, and future. This will also help determine the location of where they went missing from and where they could be going to. Accurately collecting these points is critical in knowing where we are going to start our search. Trying to predict the whereabouts of the subject, circumstances of why they are missing or lost, evaluating the terrain, environment, weather, personality, physical condition, potential or existing medical issue or abnormal behaviors will help determine a potential location or scenario.

Gathering all of this information will also assist and determine the likeliness of Detectability – the chances that the searches will be able to see the missing person in the environment in which they are lost.

Timelines are an effective tool showing events chronologically based on time.

Establishing a Starting Point

Having a basic understanding of the location of where our subject went missing from, is critical in defining the search area. There is historical data that will tell us the distance traveled by past lost persons that can be applied to the search. Understanding three key terms regarding the subject's starting position are critical. These three terms are known as Last Known Point (LKP), Point Last Seen (PLS), and Initial Planning Point (IPP).

Last Known Point (LKP) – a location or point on a map that places the subject at this particular location based on a significant clue or evidence that is related to the subject based on a well-researched subject profile.

Point Last Seen (PLS) – a location or point on the map where someone actually saw the missing subject at a specific date and time.

Initial Planning Point (IPP) – the point on the map that is used for planning the search and once the plan has initiated this point will not change unless the plan changes. IPP may be the original PLS or LKP.

Statistical distances are measured from this Initial Planning Point. Once the subject is located the distance is measured from the IPP to where the subject has been located. This information based on the subject's category can be used in statistical data for future searches.

The LKP and PLS points must be time and date-stamped to show the chronological sequence of the subject's movements. There can be many PLS and LKPs. As clues are found and validated to belong to the subject they will be marked on the map and in the field as Last Known Position (LKP).

A missing hiker may stop by a location on the trail that has a trail register. They enter their information on the trail registry that may include a date and time. This information as found by searchers would be known as the Last Known Point (LKP). While investigating this information a bystander advises you that they saw an individual meeting the description of our missing hiker would further clarify our Last Known Point (LKP) into a Point Last Seen (PLS). If this was our original point then this could end up being our Initial Planning Point (IPP) where we can apply our statistical lost person behavior distances for a hiker.

Planning and Searching Data

This initial interview will also establish planning and searching data. Planning data is information that is gathered that will assist in developing a search plan and determining the search area.

Planning Data focuses on:
- the category of the subject
- the location where they were last seen or known to be
- the circumstance of their loss
- their preparation for their trip
- their physical and mental condition
- whether currently and at the time of going missing
- there personality traits
- in the environment that they went missing in to include the terrain and the time of day

Searching data is the information that is gathered that will be provided to the searchers to allow them to know what and who they're looking for.

Searching Data focuses on:
- name to call
- physical description
- clothing description
- equipment description
- shoe print description and size
- and items that may be discarded

Searching data will identify potential clues for the searchers to look for. There are thousands of clues and only one subject. Looking for the clues will lead you to your missing subject.

Search Urgency

Interviewing the Reporting Party to collect lost person questionnaire information with emphasis on planning and searching data is critical before you can realistically apply search teams to the field. You need to know who you are looking for, what clues to look for, and what initial search tactics to apply along with establishing the priorities and urgency of the search.

The search urgency assessment was established in the late 1960s or early 1970s. Search management instructor Bill Wade helped develop the relative urgency rating system to help establish and quantify the urgency of the response to a search. Over the years since its establishment, the search urgency has assisted many agencies with quantifying the relative urgency to assist with an appropriate response based on the urgency ratings in how to conduct a search and when. Search Urgency is completed on the initial first notice but is reevaluated as time goes on and additional information is obtained.

The search urgency could change dramatically based on new information and is critical to re-evaluate especially between operational periods.

In the appendix is a copy of the search urgency form. The form is based on the evaluation and profile of nine factors:

1. Number of Subjects
2. Age
3. Medical Condition
4. Physical Condition
5. Clothing Profile
6. Equipment Profile
7. Experience Profile
8. Whether Profile
9. Terrain in Hazardous Conditions Profile

The rating is based on a score from 1 to 4 for each of the factors above with one being more concerning or urgent. Once each of the factors has been evaluated although scores are added to determine an overall rating of the relative urgency one or two factors may driver the urgency. In the overall rating or sum the lower the number the more urgent the response.

An appropriate response to the urgency ratings are as follows:

> 9-17 Urgent/Emergency Response
> 18-27 Measured Response
> 28-33 Evaluate And Investigate Response

Each agency or the authority having jurisdiction needs to determine what their level of response will be for each of these urgency ratings. No matter what the ratings are some type of response is necessary even if it's only to conduct an interview, complete the proximity search, and continue the investigation. Further investigation may provide information that would increase the urgency or help in the development of the strategy in locating the missing person.

Some agencies and jurisdictions will not order resources or send additional resources until a search urgency has been completed.

Actions So Far
You arrive on the scene based on a reporting party with the first notice that a subject is missing, you conduct an interview gathering Lost Person Questionnaire information and planning and searching data, obtained PLS, LKP point, completed a Search Urgency and did a proximity search. Now review the map of the area and determine some Reflex Tasks that can be done immediately.

Lost Person Behavior

Predictive analysis is evaluating the subject based on their behavior compared to others similar to them. By establishing a well-researched Subject Profile and understanding the behavior of the missing person may increase your chances of having a successful search. By analyzing the behavior of past lost persons, we might be able to predict what the present missing subject would do, where they may go, and where they may end up under similar circumstances. Interviewing the reporting party and others will allow us to understand the behavior in past situations allowing us to predict their current state and future state of behavior.

Searchers knowing the lost person behavior can help the searchers to understand where to look, and what to look for.

The knowledge of lost person behavior is a very powerful tool that has assisted many search managers, searchers, law enforcement, and others in having a successful search. It helps determine where to look for a lost person by evaluating distance traveled and behaviors that are typical for a particular subject category.

Many studies have been conducted as far back as the late 1960s evaluating past cases to determine common patterns of behaviors and distances traveled. These studies have found that people of certain ages with certain interests have some of the same reaction to being lost.

Lost person behavior gives searchers and planners information of what the subject might do or not do. It will also provide how far will a subject travel to and assist in determining the size of the Search Area.

Here is an overview of the research that has been completed to date:

1970 – Utah Fish and Game - Studied what do lost person's experience.

1973 – Dennis Kelly - Mountain Search for the Lost Victim - studied Southern California subjects' behavior and performance.

1977 – Bill and Jean Syrotuck - Analysis of Lost Person Behavior, Aid to Search Planning.

1983 – Barry Mitchell - Collected and reviewed 1695 cases

1984 – Ed Cornwell and Don Heth - University of Alberta – Missing Child Behavior

1995 – Bob Koester and Dave Stooksbury, University of Virginia – 245 cases studying the Behavioral Profile of Wandering Alzheimer's Patients - Alzheimer's Disease and Related Disorders SAR Research

1996 – Ed Cornwell and Don Heth - Study on how far can children could travel based on time and developed time and distance relativity charts

1997 – Dr. Kenneth Hill - Professor of Psychology at St. Mary's Univ. Nova Scotia – full review of Lost Person Behavior – Collection of Research

2008 - Bob Koester developed International Search and Rescue Incident Database (ISRID) and wrote the book "Lost Person Behavior" and assisted Chris Young and John Wehbring with their book "Urban Search" which focused on searches within the urban environment along with abduction incidents.

> By analyzing the behavior of past lost person in similar situations, you might be able to "predict" what the subject you are now looking for might do, where he might go or where he might be.
>
> This concept is a search planning tool, dealing with generalities, not absolutes.

Bob Koester's work continues to this date by collecting data from all over the world on missing person searches and once the data has been analyzed it is added to ISRID. They have also developed the Lost Person Behavior App for both Android and iPhone.

Lost Person Behavior can be its own subdiscipline. There are courses that focus on lost person behavior that are 12 to 40 hours long.

For specific details about the various characteristics and the distance traveled it is recommended downloading The Lost Person Behavior App or purchasing the Lost Person Behavior book.

Influences and Factors That May Affect a Person's Behavior

There is a difference between a lost person and a missing person. A lost person is someone who is, unable to find their way or build a cognitive map of understanding their location and how to find their way out. A small child who follows the family dog into the woods, a dementia patient who walks off from a care facility not knowing where they are going are typically a lost person.

Missing persons are typically those persons who intentionally leave, run away, or are abducted. This can include individuals that are depressed and contemplating suicide and/or the teenager who has run away from a situation at home or from school. They do not want to be found but can be harmed.

A hiker, mountain biker, rock climber, berry or mushroom picker, or an out abound skier that becomes lost has an inherent desire to be found. As a result of the inherent desire to be found they will also have the desire to survive. Just in that statement shows the type of behavior for that group of lost persons. Based on that we understand that that lost person behavior has a willingness to survive by:

- Building a fire to stay warm
- Carry equipment to survive
- Not evade searchers
- Willing to answer searchers

Assumptions of your subject based on mobility and responsiveness. We can evaluate a simple cube matrix.

	Responsive	**Unresponsive**
Mobile	Mobile / Responsive	Mobile / Unresponsive
Immobile	Immobile / Responsive	Immobile / Unresponsive

Develop Possible Scenarios based on the information gathered, the timeline, and the scenarios above and use predictions based on past lost person behavior to determine where and how to search for your missing person.

Reactions when lost

Most lost persons react immediately with astonishment and disbelief that there lost. Some will dread the embarrassment while others will panic and try to solve the problem by running in various directions or hurry up to find a familiar landmark or trail trying to implement some strategy to resolve the problem of being lost. Those with hypothermia have the behaviors of feeling warm and tend to discard clothing, not drink fluids, and discard survival equipment.

Factors that affect lost person behavior:

- **General state of health** – both from a mental and physical state can have a significant effect on their behavior. Poor physical condition, illnesses, lack of sleep, and lack of hydration can affect their behavior and survivability.
- **Personality** – their past experiences as well as their level of ego and willingness to accept help and deal with the emotional effects of being lost.
- **Day vs Night** – their behavior when they have the ability to see what's around them versus not being able to see due to darkness may affect their behavior.
- **Experience in outdoors** – the lack of experience in the outdoors would not allow them to think about survivability versus a more experienced individual who would look at building a fire, searching for water, and possible food sources.
- **Terrain, Vegetation, Weather** – when it's flat ground, very little vegetation or underbrush, and it is sunny and warm the behavior of those who are lost or changed drastically when the terrain is steep with significant vegetation, and it is wet and cold. Their ability to find trails begins to become difficult with confusion factors of barriers attractions and natural routes are eliminated.
- **Physiological effects** – when the body is affected by heat, cold, altitude, wind, wetness from precipitation in the form of rain, snow, mist, freezing rain, or ice can all have adverse effects on the body regarding hypothermia or hyperthermia affecting the brain and the ability to problem-solve.

Prevention Search and Rescue (PSAR)

There are various programs that can help educate children and outdoors enthusiasts on how to prevent becoming lost and if they do become lost what to do to survive. One of these programs is called the Hug-A-Tree program. This program started in California and was taught to kids in school on what to do if they become lost in the wilderness. The program taught to both parents as well as children teaches them about hugging a tree and staying put. They also teach kids that taking a trash bag and putting it over them as a parka will help keep their body heat in and keep them dry if it's raining. They also teach kids how to build signals using sticks, rocks, or other items so that they can be seen by helicopter. By teaching them to stay in one place and hug a tree prevents them from possibly running and panicking and injuring themselves.

Other preventative search and rescue programs include "Lost... But Found Safe and Sound" and "Lost in the Woods". The National Association for Search and Rescue is a good source for these programs.

A search and rescue team or a jurisdiction that finds they have a vulnerable population such as senior citizens living in nursing homes, assisted living residences, or senior centers may have individuals with dementia or Alzheimer's can conduct education and training on how to respond to a missing dementia or Alzheimer's patient allows them to recover them quickly.

Some of these patients along with individuals with autism may have tracking devices or bracelets. By working with the caretakers and providing them tips and education about early reporting if they go missing and searching certain areas allows for a quick recovery.

Other preventative search and rescue techniques are conducting an assessment of the search incidents in your jurisdiction and determining if there are any trends or consistent problems like a mis-marked trail or intersection. By adding maps at the trailheads or better marking a trail may help reduce or prevent a missing person search.

Any activities such as educating the public before an incident occurs or outside of the incident to prevent persons from becoming lost and if they become lost they will not what to do to survive and be easier to be located.

Chapter 6 – Clue Identification and Awareness

Objectives:

1. The student shall be able to explain why Searchers look for clues first before searching for the subject. – *ASTM F3098 (16) 12.1.2 and 12.1.3*
2. The Student shall be able to list and describe the categories of clues – *ASTM F3098 (16) 12.6.1*
3. The Student shall be able to describe why clue's life span is short.
4. The Student shall demonstrate how to mark a clue and what information they need to provide to command.
5. The Student shall know the proper procedures for handling scent articles for a search dog team
6. The Student shall know how to protect and preserve an area that a clue was located for a search dog team and/or a tracking team.
7. The Student shall understand the difference between tracking and sign-cutting.
8. The Student shall be able to describe what is clue awareness, clue oriented, and clue focus. – *ASTM F3098 (16) 12.6*

The Searcher needs to understand why clues are critical to the overall search effort. As a person walks through an area, they can leave hundreds if not thousands of clues and sign from their passing. A searcher needs to have the skills and training to know how to handle a clue but more importantly how to seek out these different types of clues and how to document and process the clue.

Searching for clues is an ongoing process by everyone from the investigator, search manager, to the searcher in the field. It starts in preplanning and continues throughout the incident and does not end until a critique is done. Clue search is a learned skill and requires practice.

An example of a training or practice session is to take a section of trail and put 10 to 15 clues of various types from clothing, tracks, discarded items, etc. and put an index card with a number and have searchers walk the trail to see if they can detect a clue. Repeated searches will increase their ability to detect items.

Lack of clues should also be considered as an important clue because it might indicate the subject was not there, false information was provided, and cause some confusion.

Good handling and processing of clues that are efficiently documented in chronological order with detailed information will ultimately help find the missing subject. The logical sequence of events, information, and/or clues will help make the search more efficient resulting in a well-managed, shorter, and safer search for everyone involved. This is where a Timeline would be beneficial.

In this next section we will cover the following items related to clues:
- Categories of Clues
- Life Span of a Clue
- Clue Awareness
- Clue Focus vs Clue Oriented

There are three key components with Clue Searching:

- **The Sensor (the Searcher)**
- **Clue Generator (the Subject)**
- **Environment (Search Area)**

The searcher is a clue seeker **(Sensor)** The sensor using recognized methods of perception, or sense is the five senses of a human: taste, sight (seeing), touch, smell, and sound (hearing). For the searcher to be effective they must be in a valid search area, have obtained Searching Data, must have been trained and qualified to locate, handle and process clues. Searchers should be well-rested and not be fatigued, as they may miss clues if tired.

The Subject is a clue **Generator** - Every person who moves through an area leaves thousands of pieces of evidence. Examples are Tracks, Scent, Discarded Materials, broken branches, crushed vegetation, etc... The Searcher must become familiar with the subject profile to differentiate between good clues and that of other searchers, people, etc...

The Search Area **(Environment)** – Define the search area, confine the search area to ensure all possible clues are within the area, and remember the environment changes over time with animals, weather, light, and other humans.

Completing a Lost Person Questionnaire will help with understanding who and what you are looking for and this will provide you with a well-research subject profile. The relationship between the Subject and the Clues found will be more reliable when a well-researched subject profile is completed.

Need to protect the Point Last Seen (PLS) and the Last Known Point (LKP). Remember to search for clues, and the subject. There are thousands of Clues but only one Subject. With the Subject being the Ultimate Clue but as a searcher, it is your responsibility to understand the clues or possible clues and understand how they related to the subject and the search. **Be Clue Aware!!**

General Clue Categories

Clues may generally be placed into the following categories:
- Physical
- Recorded
- Testimonial
- Analytical

What is a clue?

A clue is a signal or message, whose information value depends upon the sensitivity of the clue detector. A clue is a fact, an object, information, or some type of evidence that helps to solve a problem.

A tangible clue is anything the subject was wearing or carrying, including pocket contents, or other evidence the subject may leave, (Examples - a shoeprint, hat, glasses, etc.) Intangible clues would include information, sounds, or scent.

Physical
Any sign or track left on the environment by the subject such as footprints, broken brush or tree limbs, gum/candy/food wrappers, articles that may have been dropped by the subject, or human waste.

Recorded/Written
Any documentation left by the subject such as signatures at trail registers, signatures on summit logs, a written itinerary given to family or friends, a route marked on a trail map, a suicide note. ATM or purchase receipts, tag readers, cell phone records, etc.

Testimonial
Clues that are gathered through interviews and investigation are considered testimonials. Interview of witnesses, work colleagues, family, friends, or anyone who may have information about the subject is vital in building a behavioral profile of the subject. An example of a testimonial clue would be someone verbally telling you that they saw the missing subject at a specific location. This can be an important clue and it can sometimes provide a starting point for the search. Information or details provided by the reporting party could be very important and assist the search effort. Medical physician information would also be testimonial.

Analytical

Using logical reasoning and being able to separate things into their component parts in order to study or examine them, draw a conclusion, and solve problems is looking at all aspects of the search for a potential clue. Is the clue related or not?

Two types of categories exist for Analytical Clues, they are:
- Sensory
- Probable

An example of a Sensory clue would be hearing someone call out for help or smelling smoke or hearing a whistle or firearm.

Probable clues are items found that could very likely be corroborated to the lost subject. This includes clues that could conceivably belong to the lost person, but no information was provided on the Lost Person Questionnaire. No clue should be discarded or minimized but should be well documented and cataloged. No one person can adequately gather and analyze all the facts and clues.

An example of a probable clue would be a small toy found in a search for a missing child. Presently, the clue would be considered probable because it may or may not be the subject's toy, once the toy is identified by the parents it would become a physical clue. If the clue cannot be identified it is still a clue and would be probable until the resolution of the search.

Clue Life Spans

Clues do not last forever! The searcher must keep in mind that clues age over time and because of weather. Another reason why clues have limited life spans is that animals or people may disturb them.

Weather conditions will certainly play a definitive role in the life span of clues.

Wind – can blow clues from the original location to another. It can cover clues with leaves, snow, or other debris. Strong winds may actually mask the sounds of someone calling for help.

Rain – can flood or destroy tracks and other clues. Like the wind, water can move clues from their original locations and move them to another location.

Frost/ice/snow – can highlight or hide clues. Freezing temperatures may also hold the clue for a longer period of time even while aging occurs.

Heat – Can melt or evaporate certain clues. The clue may reflect the light to make it easier to see.

Time is a searchers' worst enemy. It will deteriorate and destroy the clue the longer it is exposed to the elements.

Wildlife – may carry clues away, move clues, bury or eat clues as well as People (non-searchers) - move clues, picking up or throwing away clues, may contaminate clues with their scent when touching or handling the clue. Most people will not be able to show you exactly where they found the clue.

The subject who is still in the area will continue to generate clues especially their sent, tracks, and discarded items.

Clue Awareness and Clue Orientation

Clue awareness is the searcher's ability to identify and search for objects that are unnatural and unusual to the environment. Deciphering why is this clue here.

Clue Awareness is having the knowledge, skill, and ability through training and experience to understand:
- The importance of clues to the overall search effort
- Why do we search for clues first, then the subject
- Which clues could possibly be found that could be left by the subject
- How and where to search for different categories of clues
- To understand what clues could be yielded during night searches
- How to handle, process, and manage clues that are found
- The lack of clues is also a clue and understanding why it is important.

Understanding clues is important. Another term used is known as **SIGN**. Signs which are changes in the natural state of the environment such as dew on the grass in the morning but footsteps will disrupt or change the natural state. So, any evidence of change from the natural state that is inflicted on the environment is known as sign.

Clues – Are objects or facts that may help us to solve a problem or mystery They can be visual or not visual (scent)

Sign – Any evidence of change from the natural state that is inflicted on the environment indicating the passing of the missing subject. This can include bruising, breakage, change of color, disturbance, flattening, scuff, or shine of the environment.

Clue Awareness – Awareness level that all searchers and search managers should have regarding the evaluation and importance of clues and how they should handle the clue or sign once found. The location of a clue may help to determine the missing person's location or direction of travel, or both.

What Do We Do If We Find a Clue

Before leaving base or the command post to go to your search assignment, the searcher or the team leader should obtain information on how to handle the clues or sign found. A basic procedure and process are as follows:

1. Notify Command
   a. Give Description of Clue or Sign
   b. GPS Location/ Map Coordinates (USNG)

2. Command Will Decide What To Do With Clue
   a. They will advise the next step if they think the clue is relevant

3. Document Location – Flag area.
   a. Photograph – careful – ask permission
   b. Sketch
   c. GPS Location
   d. Flag area (mark flag with pertinent info)
   e. Collect clue if instructed to do so by command

Do not disturb the clue unless directed to do so by command. Command is usually the call sign of the Incident Command Post (ICP).

The Area where the clue is found should be treated as the Last Known Point (LKP) and the area should be **protected** from any future disturbance or damage. Preserve the area, trails, and the sign or clue for the tracking team and the K9s. Be conscious of how your team arrived into the area.

Command will log the clue on the clue log with date/time/location/description of clue/and who located the clue. They will also determine the Clue number which is the day of the month and the sequential number of clues found that day. An example is Clue -12-02.

The Searcher and their team as well as management will decide if the clue is relevant. This is where the well-researched subject profile comes into play to validate the clue.

Command will determine the next action to be taken by the searcher such as to wait for another resource like a bloodhound or an evidence collection team or for the Searcher or Team to collect or leave the clue in place. Most clues will be processed and collected by law enforcement. No matter what the information will be documented and the site will be marked.

The search team should do a proximity search to ensure the subject is not sitting close by just out of sight. Additionally, looking for sign or tracks leading to and from the clue will help with the direction of travel.

Before checking or searching for an additional sign, tracks, or clues in an area where a clue was located make sure it is safe to search. If the missing subject is found but is injured whatever caused their injuries could also injure or harm the searchers. Make sure the scene or area is safe. Do a 360 search and look at the surroundings.

Marking of a Clue

It requires three arms length strips of flagging tape. On one of the strips of flagging tape write with a permanent marker the following information

- Date
- Time
- Resource/Team ID
- USNG Coordinates
- Clue Log #
- Task #
- Broad Description

3/24/2009   17:45   MSP K9-2   O128/9973   Clue# 24-3   Task 24-62 "Shoe"

Once locating a clue or sign it can give us a lot of information such as location, time, elevation, the direction of travel, intent, and corroboration of the story of our missing person. If the subject is located first identify if the scene is safe, conduct an assessment, provide first aid and/or CPR. If the subject is deceased treat the area as a crime scene by preserving the scene and area and keeping people away including other team members until law enforcement arrives.

Clues are messages. Understanding how they relate is critical. Clues can tell us the present location of the subject, where the subject was, where the subject is going, what the subject is doing, and where the subject was not. Where the subject is not is based on searching several search areas and finding nothing may establish that the subject was not there. The location of numerous clues can develop a timeline and direction of travel.

Search is a Classic Mystery and as searchers, we have to think with an open mind and be looking for all types of search objects, changes in the environment, changes in behavior, etc.

You must know what clues to look for, possible destination ascertained, and recreate the circumstances of the incident or possible triggers that may cause the person to go missing or get lost. Triggers may be being delayed from a hike and the sunsets and their hike is in the dark with a changing environment. Other triggers may be an argument, falling behind, not paying attention, breaking up, loss of a job, change in medical condition, or financial overburden. These triggers lead us to various search objectives to look for.

Search is tied to Law Enforcement Investigation since police have the resources, training, investigative skills, and the jurisdiction and responsibility to manage a missing or lost person. They can conduct cell phone analysis, computer, and social media analysis which can provide certain clues or their whereabouts.

Law Enforcement Agency for the jurisdiction is known as the Responsible Agency or Authority. They should be responsible for the interview and investigation. A Search Manager may participate in the interview.

Always remember that the investigation is a Never-ending Process. Once we find the individual an interview and investigation will continue to answer the question of what happened and why?

Never discount the possibility of a criminal act – the incident could end up as a staged incident, homicide, kidnapping or abduction, abuse, runaway, and/or suicidal. Searchers should know how to preserve the chain of evidence at any search. A clue or search object should be treated as a piece of evidence because you will not know until you find your lost or missing person or the conclusion of the investigation.

The investigation and interview will get you basic information on the type of subject and the clues to be looking for. It will also determine if the missing subject will respond if their name is called, the chance of survivability, their ability to travel, and how they will travel.

Preserving the Area and clues for K9's

Working with a scent discriminating search dog requires search teams to preserve the Last Know Position (LKP) and the Point Last Seen (PLS) as a starting point for the scent discriminating search dog. Keep the area clear of people and disturbance to ensure the most optimal conditions for the trackers and scent discriminating search dogs.

This would include keeping vehicles, ATVs, or other motorized units from the area to prevent contaminating the area with exhaust fumes.

When securing or obtaining a scent article for the scent discriminating search dog the article should have been previously or most recently touched or worn by the subject. Such items may be a pillowcase, hairbrush, or clothing from the hamper. Always use rubber gloves to handle the article and keep the articles separate by placing them in different bags and do not allow them to touch each other which may cause cross-contamination. Place separated articles inside of clear plastic or evidence bags (do not use a standard trash bag because of the deodorizers that are used in them which can mask the scent for the canine). A plain paper bag will work.

Notes and summary:

A well-researched subject profile will help make clues more reliable.

General Categories of Clues: Analytical, Testimonial, Physical, and Recorded.

Find a clue and it relates to your missing person treat as the Last Know Point (LKP).

As time passes clues will be destroyed by weather, non-trained searchers, and the subject may leave new clues.

Remember the Crucial: Search for Clues, and the subject because there is only one subject and thousand clues.

Searchers that are not clue-aware can destroy clues.

Chapter 7 – Philosophy of Search Planning

Objectives:
1. The student shall know the following terms and understand their significance in a search operation: *ASTM F3098 (16) - 12.3*
   - Search Segment and Search Area
   - Probability of Area (POA)
   - Probability of Detection (POD)
   - Probability of Success (POS)
   - Coverage
2. The student shall know the factors that affect coverage and POD. *ASTM F3098 (16) - 12.4*
3. The student shall demonstrate an understanding of the basic principles affecting search operations and be able to list the fundamental Crucial's to search operations. *ASTM F3098 (16) - 12.1*
4. The student shall have a basic understanding of search theory and how it is applied to a missing person search

Dennis Kelly, author of the classic search and rescue book called *Mountain Search for the Lost Victim* and a pioneer in search management and search theory. Based on his work with Montrose Search and Rescue Team in Southern California he coined the phrase ***Search is an Emergency***. In the early 1970s after responding to many searches in the National Park Service along with many others in search management collectively developed the **"Crucial's"** for search operations".

These collective principles and best practices have helped drive successful searches and remind those that are managing or searching for a missing person of the critical components that are necessary for a successful search.

Over the years they have been revised and expanded upon. But for the purposes of this book, we will stay focused on the original six Crucial's.

> ## The Crucials:
>
> - Search is an emergency.
> - Search is a classic mystery.
> - Search for clues, and the subject.
> - Concentrate on the aspects that are:
>   - important to search success
>   - under the control of a search manager
> - Know if the subject leaves the search area
> - Grid Search is used as a last resort

Crucial's of Search Operations

1. **Search is an EMERGENCY**
   The subject may:
   - need emergency care.
   - need protection from self and environment.
   - only will be responsive for a few hours/days.
   - Time and weather destroy clues.
   - An urgent response lessens search difficulty.
   - Urgent response permits the use of more efficient search techniques.
   - Response level measured by Search Urgency.

2. **Search is a Classical Mystery**
   - You must know what clues to look for.
   - Possible destinations ascertained.
   - Circumstances of the incident re-created.
   - The subject may return home or show up at a friend's house.
   - Point Last Seen (PLS) or Last Known Position (LKP) identified.
   - Distance compared with subject behavior data. (from IPP)

3. **Search for Clues, and the subject**
   There may be hundreds, if not thousands of clues...and only one subject. Every missing subject will leave clues and "sign" as evidence of their passage through an area. As time passes new clues are left.

   Detecting clues will substantially reduce the search difficulty.

4. **Concentrate on aspects that are:**
   - Important to the Search Success - Finding Subject
   - Under The control of the Search Manager
     - Assure Unity of Command
     - Crews must function together as a crew with a crew leader
     - The chain of command goes from Crew Leader to Operations Chief to Incident Commander
     - Leaders and followers can make this happen
     - Use Checklists and a Qualified Search Manager

5. **Know if the subject leaves the search area. *CONFINE!***
   - Understand that confinement is a "crucial" part of the search
   - Do this with the same dedication as any other function
   - Searching an area that doesn't contain the subject is a waste of time.

6. **Grid Search is used as a last resort.**
   - Requires vast numbers of searchers
   - Can look only for subjects if untrained
   - Destroys Clues and evidence
   - Takes a long time to cover an area
   - Inefficient and management intensive

Concentrate on finding the subject

DO NOT WORRY ABOUT
- Are we in the wrong place?
- Is this the right tactic?
- What kind of resource is used
- Who is going to find the subject

History and Background of Search Theory

Operations Research (OR) is a professional scientific discipline that provides for a systematic approach to informed decision-making, especially in uncertain situations as a missing person search.

Search Theory is an applied mathematical sub-discipline of Operation Research (OR) that uses OR principles and methods to help resolve search problems. In short, search theory is a mathematical approach to determining how best to find what we are searching for: Missing Persons, Gold, Oil, Mineral, archeology, etc.

In our situation, we are looking for a missing person and associated clues left by the missing person in a predetermined geographical area or region. This geographical area or region is typically known as our Initial Search Area (ISA).

History of Search Theory: Benard O. Koopman (1900-1981), a Harvard educated scientist, established the basis for a rigorous study of search theory and practice with his pioneering work for the U.S. Navy during World War II.

The work initially done by Koopman and colleagues was instrumental in the Allied approach to the Battle of the Atlantic and antisubmarine warfare. You may say what does this have to do with searching for a missing person and how does this affect me. The basic theory of search established by Koopman applies to all types of searching, including that of inland search and searching for a missing person. Search Theory is applied today in our military in Iraq and Afghanistan and used to find missing aircraft and boaters. His contribution has helped us where we are to look today and the effectiveness of looking for the missing person.

The United States Coast Guard provided the first comprehensive application to civil search and rescue in the 1950s and was incorporated into the US National Search and Rescue Manual in 1959. The point is that Operation Research is a proven well used systematic approach to finding missing objects and some key search theory concepts are used by field personnel and can significantly improve communications between them and the search planners and managers who are using this concept to plan the search.

Operations Research (OR) - A professional scientific discipline providing for a systematic approach to informed decision-making.

Search Theory - An applied mathematical sub-discipline of OR and uses OR principles and methods to resolve search problems.

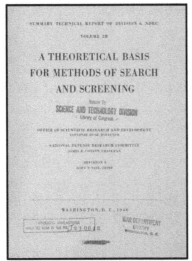

https://www.loc.gov/resource/dcmsiabooks.theoreticalbasis02koop/?sp=7&r=-1.005,-0.574,3.011,2.54,0

Bernard O. Koopman: USA WW II research to sink U-Boats. Bayesian statistics & probability developing Detection index or sweep width.

Search Probabilities

Search probabilities will assist us in determining the most likely search area to search and once we have searched an area it will provide us with the probability of what we were able to detect. Search probabilities will allow us to determine our coverage given as an objective probability of detection and will allocate our resources effectively to achieve the ultimate outcome of finding a missing person.

It is important to understand that a search requires a missing subject within a defined search area. We need to understand how to determine where to search.

We discussed the various points of Point Last Seen (PLS), Last Known Point (LKP), and Initial Planning Point (IPP) in Chapter 5.

Search Area Establishment

A very important step in developing a search plan is identifying where the subject went missing from and where are they possibly going. The crucial step in determining where to search is a process called Search Area Establishment which is done using four basic methods in sequential order.

> ### Search Area Establishment
> Four Methods to developing a Search Area:
> 1. **Theoretical**
> 2. **Statistical**
> 3. **Subjective**
> 4. **Deductive**

Search Area or Initial Search Area - the "search area" is the physical geographic area that the search planner believes is likely to contain the search object. In determining the search area is critical to consider the missing persons last known point (LKP) or point last seen (PLS), their intended destination, possible or likely routes, past historical search data of the area, lost person behavior characteristics, and distances traveled by past lost persons. The Initial Search Area (ISA) is the initial area to be searched. This area will be broken down into search segments.

Time is a major factor in determining the search area. Knowing the exact time when the subject went missing to the current time gives us a period of time which they have been missing.

Theoretical - Depending on how fast the subject could move multiplied by the period of time which they have been missing gives us our **Theoretical Search Area.** An average person takes about 20 minutes to walk 1 mile. Or walks 3 miles per hour (MPH). If the subject has been missing for two hours the subject could go in any direction up to 6 miles. Knowing they can go in any direction to get our theoretical search area we use the formula of PI (π) or 3.14 X radius $(R)^2$. The search area can be 113 sq. miles. This is known as the theoretical search area. It is critical to respond early and quickly and apply confinement search tactics to lessen the size of the search area.

Statistical – Looking at the lost person behavior data which has statistical distances traveled by other past lost persons gives use the statistical distance data in quartiles such as 25%, 50%, 75%, and 95% with 5% being the outlier for those who travel further beyond the statistical range.

Subjective – When applying the Theoretical and Statistical information to a Topographical or orthophoto (aerial photograph) map it allows the search manager to see the limiting factors such as cliffs, barriers, attractions, trails, open areas, water boundaries, streams/rivers, etc. So, any feature that can affect or influence the subject's travel and behavior. Likely Spots.

Deductive Reasoning – The analysis of all the information such as searching and planning data, information on the Lost Person Questionnaire, and the lost person behavior brought together to develop possible scenarios and locations in combination with the Theoretical, Statistical, and Subjective information.

Once the Theoretical and Statistical Range Rings are on the map and Subjective and Deductive Reasoning is completed the Initial Search Area (ISA) is the initial area that needs to be drawn or outlined on the map to define the search area for the initial or first operational period. This area will need to be divided up into searchable segments for search teams to search. Also, the Probability of Area can be applied. This is where mapping comes into play.

Search Segment - is an area that is segmented or subdivided from the search area based on the logistical and operational issues associated with conducting the search itself. Search segments are based on the searcher or search resource that is assigned to search that segment based on their capabilities and time. A segment should be small enough that it can be searched by the intended search resource with a reasonable coverage in a specified amount of time.

Typically, a search segment that can be searched by an air-sent K-9 team or a six-person ground team will normally be less than 100 acres and they are given a timeframe of 3 to 4 hours. Understanding time and distance at walking speed will take an average person 1 minute and 15 seconds to walk approximately

328 feet or 100 meters. With this information, we can calculate the approximate time to search 100 acres of area which is approximately 3.5 hours or 210 minutes.

Each search segment should have a clear definitive boundary such as a road, trail, opening to a clearing, stream, geographic features such as a cliff, Ridgeline, or Valley.

Probability of Area (POA) - the probability that the search object or missing subject is contained within the boundaries of an area or segment.

Probability of Detection (POD) – the probability of the search object being detected, assuming it was in the areas that were searched. POD is the function of coverage factor, sensor, search conditions, and the accuracy with which the search unit navigates its assigned search pattern. Measures the sensor effectiveness under the prevailing search conditions.

Probability of Success (POS) – the probability of finding the search object with a particular search. The Probability of Area (POA) X The Probability of Detection (POD) = the Probability of Success (POS).

Coverage - measures how thoroughly a search team searched or covered the assigned search segment. Coverage takes the area effectively swept and compares it to the physical area of the entire segment assigned. Coverage is a value described as a ratio. Coverage of one indicates that the assigned segment was effectively swept or searched by the search team.

$$\text{Coverage} = \frac{\text{Area Effectively Searched (Swept)}}{\text{Area of the Search Segment}}$$

When searching a segment, vegetation, terrain, and the target characteristics most definitely impact coverage.

Once you have the coverage you can then calculate The Probability of Detection (POD). In the appendix is a POD versus coverage chart.

POD = 1 – e^{-c}

Z = Area Effectively Swept
A = Area to be covered
C = Coverage

$$C = \frac{Z}{A} = \frac{0.18 squaremiles}{0.25 squaremiles} = 0.72$$

Based on the example above our coverage was .72 when this is mathematically calculated based on the formula above our probability of detection is 52%.

Briefing and Debriefing:

As a search team, it is critical to receive your assignment and briefing of what is expected of you while searching your specific assigned search segment. This would include obtaining a task assignment sheet and search segment map. This task assignment will clearly identify the amount of time your team has to accomplish searching the segment that your team has been assigned. When your team has completed their search and you have returned to the command post you will report your overall findings during the debriefing. This is necessary to extract the relevant and pertinent information from the search team to ensure the effectiveness of the search. Most debriefings are conducted in writing but there are cases where this is done verbally.

Below is a copy of a debriefing checklist. This debriefing checklist has various items that will help quantify the description of the area covered and help determine coverage which ultimately becomes Probability of Detection (POD).

Some of the items covered are as follows:
- Estimated forward search speed
- The exact length of time spent searching
- Field measurements of Range of Detection (RD) or some similar field-observable measure
- Other field-observable measures identified and requested before the assignment
- Qualitative description of the search
- Qualitative description of the search conditions
- the exact location of clues located regardless of how insignificant and their disposition.

DEBRIEFING CHECKLIST

Time task completed: _____	Name of Debriefer: _____
Date / Time prepared: _____	Total Time actually searching: _____
Time Searching Started: _____	Time Searching Stopped:_____
How Many Searchers on Team: _____ How far apart was spacing: _____ (Ft.)	
The Size of the Seach Area **Searched**: _____ (Acres) _____ (Sq. Kilometers)	

TEAM PERFORMANCE:
Visibility / weather conditions: _____
Terrain conditions: _____ Hazards noted: _____
Was task completed as assigned? YES NO *IF NO, explain*:_____
_____
Average Maximum Detection Range (AMDR) _____(FT) Total Track Line Length: _____ (Ft)
Qualitative Description of Search (Poor, Average, Great): **Narrative**_____
Estimate of forward Speed of Search (Fast, Normal, Slow): _____
Was there any gaps in the area searched? YES NO *If Yes, explain*: _____
Was the team adequately equipped?   YES NO *If NO, explain*: _____
Was the team's composition adequate?   YES NO *If NO, explain*: _____
Was the team's performance adequate?   YES NO *If NO, explain*: _____
Is the team's morale adequate?   YES NO *If NO, explain*: _____
Is the team ready for another task? YES NO *If NO, explain*: _____
Did the team use a GPS? YES NO *If Yes, Did Debriefer download data?* _____

The Probability of Detection (POD) does provide a way to estimate the successfulness of the search area and provides a way for the search team to evaluate its performance.

There are some key terms in determining or calculating coverage such as track line and Sweep Width.

Track Line is the path or route taken by a search resource that moves through a segment. Track Line Length is the length of the path that a resource took while it was searching in a designated segment.

The conservative visual range for detection also known as Range of Detection (RD) is determined by the size and color of the target, the sensor, terrain, vegetation, and other environmental conditions at the time of the search along the track line.

Since there are no land search sweep width tables, sweep width has to be estimated based on the environmental factors of the area. This visual range equals your Sweep Width. Average Maximum Detection Range (AMDR) was a previous technique but Range Detection (RD) replaced AMDR. Many studies have been completed on Sweep Width and the most effective technique is the use of Range Detection (RD). The technique is placing an object or person close in similarity to the missing person in clothing color, size, and description. Searchers will walk away from the object in 8 cardinal directions till they cannot see the object or person, turn around walk back till they see the object, and Stop. Measure the distance back to the object using pace counting. Do this for each of the 8 cardinal directions. The average of the 8 distances will be your Range Detection (RD) or the sweep width.

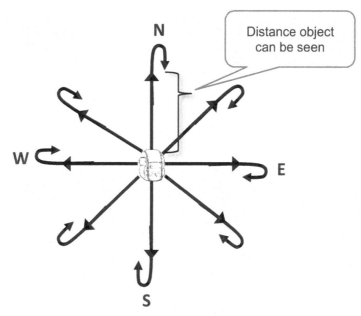

Sweep Width (**W**) X Track Line length (**TLL**) = Area Effectively Swept (**Z**)

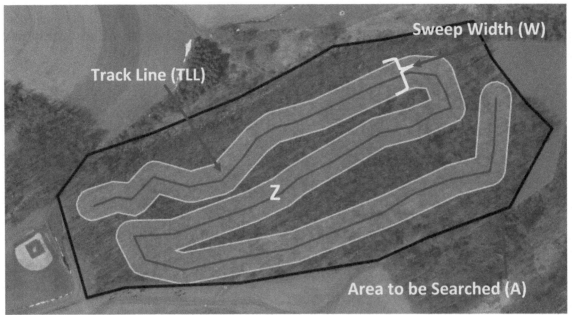

Coverage is using Sweep Width and Trackline Length to get the area effectively swept, then this is divided by the Search Area Assigned.

Jack R. Frost, a well-known search theorist with the United States Coast Guard (USCG) outlined that there are four groups of variables that can affect the probability of detection (POD):

- the sensor
- the search object
- the environment
- the method of searching

Factors Affecting Performance

Many factors can affect the motivation and performance of the searchers. These factors can distract the searcher or sensor from detecting a search object or missing person. Some of these factors are:

- Weather, terrain, vegetation
- Time of day
- Searcher Fatigue
- Searcher Expectations
- Searcher Training
- Poor Leadership

Chapter 8 – Search Resources

Objectives:

1. The Student shall be able to list at least 5 types of operational resources that can be used in search operations.
2. The Student shall be able to understand and describe the six basic questions of evaluating a resource.
3. The Student shall be able to describe the advantages and disadvantages of two types of resources.

This is an introduction to the types of resources that may be used during a SAR incident. It is the Local jurisdiction's responsibility to evaluate SAR resources that may be utilized. The Search manager has the responsibility to select the best resources and use them correctly for each incident.

In Chapter 10, The Search Team and SAR Organizations will cover various types of organizations and the make-up of a search team. Resources can be categorized as Human/Animal, Equipment/Technology, and Informational.

Ab Taylor, an experienced search manager, and tracker stated that large numbers of searchers do not improve a search nor does money but a small group of well-trained searchers directed by a qualified search manager is far more superior to a large number of untrained searchers. One reason is that Grid Search is not effective or efficient.

When reviewing resources, it is important to understand that what finds the missing person is the sensor. The sensor may be visual via eyes, or enhanced with cameras like high resolution or forward-looking infrared (FLIR), or night vision goggles. The sensor may be smell using K-9's to sniff scent. Understanding the platforms that carry these important sensors and placing the platform in the right place at the right time to detect the signal or scent is what locates the missing subject. Platforms are aircraft, drones, equines, vehicles, towers, K9s, watercraft, or humans.

Types of Resources for Search and Rescue

Aviation

There are several types of SAR resources in the aviation sector. These are very specialized resources that may not be available due to mechanical issues, climatic conditions, or location as related to restricted air space. Helicopters and fixed-wing aircraft come with a high cost per hour to operate and agreements with organizations who provide these resources should be in place before being requested.

Helicopters

Helicopters may be a versatile resource. They can be used to transport SAR resources, medical personnel and even the subject should circumstances require. As a search platform, they can "hover" over an area that is unique to helicopters. Some helicopters are equipped with searching tools such as Forward-Looking Infrared, night vision, and searchlights. If the crew is trained in SAR operations, they can provide a unique perspective to a visual search. It must be stated, not all helicopters and crews are equipped and/or trained in search operations.

Drones – Small Unmanned Aerial Systems (sUAS)

Much like helicopters, sUAS can provide a unique perspective during search operations. There are many types of sUAS platforms that provide different abilities and results to the search. An sUAS team should be trained specifically for SAR operations. Much like the helicopter, The sUAS platform can be fitted with various sensors, standard video, Forward-looking Infrared, and thermal. The area that an sUAS can cover is significantly smaller especially with the limitation of power and elevation.

Fixed Wing Aircraft

Fixed-wing aircraft are most commonly used for searches over large areas. Smaller fixed-wing aircraft can fly "low and slow" over the search area conducting a visual search. Some aircraft are equipped to detect and track electronic emergency locator beacons. They can also provide transportation and communication services. Just like the helicopter, the crew must be trained in SAR operations to be an effective platform.

Search and Rescue Dogs.

Dogs are trained for many jobs; Service, Therapy, Hunting, Drug and explosive detection, tracking, air-scenting, Cadaver, etc. We are going to focus on dogs in search and rescue. The most commonly used dogs for SAR are Tracking, Trailing and Air Scent.

Humans constantly give off scent that becomes airborne. Shedding skin cells that can travel large distances in the air or pass through tiny cracks, porous materials, or crevices, and are even carried through water lifting the scent into the air. Below we will outline these two types of K9s, their capabilities, and their limitations.

Canines are used in search operations for water searches, wilderness, and wooded area searches, human remains detections (cadaver), avalanche, disaster, or collapse buildings.

Air Scent dog - Air scent dogs do not need a PLS and can start from anywhere in a search area. The air scent dog works the wind with raised head seeking to locate generic human scent. A SAR dog does not work on lead, will range out in front of their handler as the team moves through their assigned search area.

Tracking dog – Tracking dogs will typically work on lead and will mostly have their nose to the track following ground disturbance. A good tracking dog will be able to work through a variety of terrain. Most tracking dogs work on lead and typically are police K9.

Trailing dog - A trailing dog is *scent specific*, may also have his/her head up using some of the air scent techniques to find the subject. Trailing dogs will usually work on lead, they may venture off the actual path that a subject took due to the wind blowing the scent or a scent pool may be discovered. They are following a specific scent and working through all other human scents to get to the source.

The understanding scent of various types and how that scent moves and forms a cone of scent is important to the search team and search managers. Winds and terrain will affect the scent travel along with atmospheric conditions such as humidity, moisture, and hot or cold temperatures.

Equine

A search and rescue horse team are trained and used to perform mounted search and rescue. In some cases, the horse is simply a means of

transportation for a SAR responder. The horse can also be a full member of the SAR field team. A mounted SAR resource pays close attention to the horses' senses of hearing, scenting, and vision. A mounted SAR resource has a very different perspective than a person walking in the same area. Riders and horses are trained to safely and effectively perform the search function as a team.

Search Teams

People can be trained to be effective sensors to locate the subject and to provide medical and rescue assistance to the subject when located. It is important to note that many first responders, such as law enforcement and firefighters, are not necessarily trained in urban or wilderness search. Utilizing qualified SAR teams is crucial to a successful search. Qualified SAR teams are certified through a Nationally recognized organization. Search teams can be grid search teams, human trackers, and hasty search teams.

As a ground SAR team, a searcher uses all of their senses, sight, smell, hearing, even touch to locate clues and the subject. SAR teams are trained in many search tactics such as Rapid (Hasty), Efficient, containment, and thorough searches. These tactics will be further discussed in Chapter 9.

Grid Teams – can involve 5 to 20 members depending on experience but remember more individuals searching in a grid or concentrated area does mean it is effective or efficient. There are two types of grids search teams first is loose open-spaced grid teams known as an efficient grid search team and the second is a tight closed-spaced thorough grid search team. Some of the grid search teams are made up of self-organizing, "emergent" voluntary groups and individuals that are willing to help. But they have no formal training, experience, or preparation for the outdoors.

Always remember the crucial – *"Grid Search is Used as a Last Resort"*. A large-scale search of untrained resources can hamper or hinder a search making it inefficient and a logistical burden.

Human trackers or mantracking is another type of search team that follows the track of the subject by finding "sign" or tracks (footprints). Signs are disturbances left by the subject moving through an area such as footprints and trampled vegetation. This work takes patients and a keen eye.

Hasty Search Teams are used as a first resource to check out high probability areas quickly. Hasty Search Teams are a group of two to three searchers that is highly trained, self-sufficient, and have pinpoint navigational skills. Hasty Search Teams utilize fast, thorough search tactics in areas most likely to produce clues or the subject themselves. Searchers should understand the equipment they use to enhance their senses. Hasty Search Teams use a variety of search tactics and can conduct purposeful wandering looking at potential avenues the subject may have taken.

All Search Teams will have a Team Leader, Navigator, and a radio operator. All search teams should have either a 12 or 24 hour backpack with survival, equipment, clothing, or other gear like personal protective equipment (PPE), rain gear, and clothing.

Technical Rescue/Medical Teams

There are specialized search and rescue teams such as water rescue, technical rope rescue, cave, and mine rescue, urban and disaster USAR search and rescue, and Avalanche SAR Teams. Water rescue resources are trained and equipped to respond to searches in Tidal or surf, swift-water in rivers and streams, floodwaters, and open waters of ponds and lakes.

These teams involved in water rescue have specific training in these environments and conditions and require good swimming and boating skills. They will have various types of equipment such as dive or SCUBA gear. The water environment can be very dangerous and requires everyone working near, in, or around the water to wear a Type 3 personal floatation device (PFD).

Technical rope units are equipped for steep mountainous areas. Confined space teams are equipped for situations in mines, caves, collapsed structures, and other situations involving confined space.

A discussion and additional information of where resources can be obtained from and how to evaluate the team or resources will be in Chapter 10.

Sensor resources:
- Thermal Imaging Cameras
- Forward-Looking Infrared
- Sonar
- Sound or Vibration Devices
- GPS Units

These units or devices enhance the human senses to be able to see, hear, or know better.

Communications (radios, frequency, ham/amateur radio)

Communication is crucial to the SAR operation. Several organizations provide support for SAR incidents. The ability to communicate to SAR resources during an incident is frequently managed by a communication unit. This function handles radio frequencies and possible deployment of mobile repeaters and handheld radios. They manage most if not all radio traffic during an incident.

Search Management

The management of a SAR incident is crucial to a successful search. The most recognized position is the Incident Commander, who may also serve as a Search Manager. Plans, Operations, Investigation, and Public Affairs and also specialized positions in the search organization. On most missing person search operations, a law enforcement agency will assign an officer as the Incident Commander and the Search Manager may be a technical advisor to the Incident Commander.

The Incident Commander (IC) is responsible for all decisions and activities during a search. Using the ICS template, the incident staff can expand as necessary during an incident. An investigation is the foundation of every SAR incident. It is probably the most important function directly related to finding the subject. It determines the subject category, the IPP, the search area and is an ongoing operation throughout the entire incident.

Planning collects, evaluates, disseminates information about the incident. Plans oversee all incident-related data gathering and analysis regarding incident operations and assigned resources, develop alternatives for tactical operations, conduct planning meetings, and prepare the Incident Action Plan (IAP) for each operational period. Public affairs formulate and release information to news and social media with the approval of the IC.

Investigators and Interviewers

We will further discuss the investigation because of the importance of this function. An investigation is an ongoing activity throughout the entire incident. It is critical and vital to the success of the search incident. Investigators are working to learn about the subject through interviews with friends and family. In exigent circumstances, law enforcement can obtain information from cell phones, credit card activity, and video systems that may lead to valuable data about the subject. Investors create a timeline of events related to the subject leading up to and during the incident, building an understanding of events.

The investigation is continuous throughout the search. Collecting critical information and developing timelines will determine where the subject may be or where they could have gone. Also, understanding the reason why the individual went missing.

Electronic distress indicating devices

A distress signal indicates that a person or group of people, ship, aircraft, or other vehicle is threatened by serious and/or imminent danger and requires immediate assistance. There are three types of electronic beacons used to transmit distress signals:

- *Emergency Position Indicating Radio Beacon* (EPIRB) is used in maritime applications.
- *Emergency Locator Transmitter* (ELT) is designed for use in aircraft. These two types of transmitters can be automatically or manually activated.
- *Personal Locator Beacon* (PLB). It is designed to be carried by an individual such as hikers and climbers. Unlike the EPIRB and ELT, the PLB can only be activated manually.

All of these devices are part of the COSPAS-SARSAT Program. Cospas-Sarsat is an international, humanitarian search and rescue system that uses satellites to detect and locate emergency beacons carried by ships, aircraft, or individuals. The system consists of a network of satellites, ground stations, mission control centers, and rescue coordination centers.

Specialized aircraft and ground teams equipped and trained on the use of handheld locating devices are used to detect and locate these electronic devices.

Other Public Safety Resources

Fire and Rescue Agencies like the local rescue squad, the fire department, and the emergency medical service can provide rescue capabilities following the NFPA 1006 and 1670 standards at the awareness, operations, and technician levels. Many of the Fire and Rescue Departments have special technical rescue teams that can conduct technical rescues, disaster searches and provide emergency medical care in a rescue or difficult situation.

Law Enforcement Agencies have specialized teams for man-tracking, evidence search teams, and tactical medical teams. Tactical Medical Teams can provide emergency medical care in a very dangerous or hostile environment at the advanced medical care level.

Chapter 9 – Tactical Search Operations

Objectives:

1. The student should be able to describe each of the components of search operations.

2. The student shall know the differences between active (or direct) and passive (or indirect) search tactics, there are advantages and disadvantages, and the reason for their use. *ASTM F3098 (16) 12.7*

3. The student shall know how the passive or indirect search tactics of investigation, attraction, and containment are performed. *ASTM F3098 (16) 12.8*

4. The Student shall be able to explain and demonstrate the differences of the following active or direct search tactics: *ASTM F3098 (16) 12.9*

    a. Type I – hasty search

    b. Type II – loose, area, sweep, or efficient search

    c. Type III– tight, grade, evidence, or thorough search.

5. The student shall have a basic understanding of tracking or sign cutting that could be used in search operations. *ASTM F2099 (14) 12.10 and 12.11*

6. The student should understand how to preserve an area and the proper procedures for handling sent articles for a search dog. *ASTM F3098 (16) 12.11 and 12.12*

7. The student shall know the advantages and disadvantages of nighttime searching. *ASTM F3098 (16) 12.15*

8. The student shall know the functions of the Search Team Leader, Radio Operator, Navigator, and Search Teams Members. *ASTM F3098 (16) 12.5*

The search operation components also known as the six phases of search and rescue operation will flow in a continuous state. These components were discussed earlier in chapter 1.

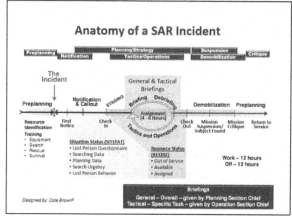

- **Preplanning** – is the preparation and planning before an incident occurs. This will include training, gathering equipment, establishing standard operating procedures, and testing equipment for its readiness. It allows searchers to be both mentally and physically prepared for a mission.

- **Notification** – this can be the notification that someone's missing and the notification to the SAR teams to respond to an incident. Most critically is the notification by the reporting party to the responsible agency. Once the evaluation and urgency are rated notification to start teams will occur.

- **Planning and Strategy** – this is the process of gathering the information collecting the searching and planning data, evaluating the urgency, and reviewing the lost person behavior. This is also developing the strategic plan for operations including ordering resources and establishing a check-in. The planning phase is also ongoing and dynamic as new situational information is received and interpreted. This phase is normally handled by the planning section chief.

- **Tactics and Operations** – as resources arrive they will check-in, receive a briefing, and be placed in staging until their tactical assignment can be given to them through a tactical briefing. The majority of the tactical work is conducted in the Operations Section and accomplished by the resources searching their assigned search segments. Resources are tracked. This is where planned strategies are tactically carried out. The Operation Section Chief is responsible for carrying out the planned tactical assignments. Tactics is an action to achieve an objective.

When resources are completed an assignment they will return to command to be debriefed by the Planning Section. This ensures good and quality feedback from the searchers. Resources will then await for an additional assignement in the Staging area.

- **Suspension** – the operation is finally discontinued, whether or not it is successful. When it is not successful A Limited Continuous Search is performed which is when the mission is suspended but not the search. The search continues on a limited basis while the investigation continues as an open missing person's case. During this phase the process of demobilization and check out is completed.
  - **Demobilization** - is the process of returning all equipment, materials, and personnel back to their original ready status, replacing and restoring all used equipment and materials, and ensuring the safe return of all personnel. It is also the process of releasing resources from the incident. This process start when you call your first resource or they are mobilized.

- **Critique** – a mission critique allows for a thorough evaluation of the operations with input from searchers. It is a total evaluation of the searchers, methods, and strategies used during the operations an **"Inclusive Evaluation"**. The most important aspect is learning from our strengths and weaknesses reevaluating new strategies and preplanning for the next event. There are operational, organizational, and personal critiques. Above outlines the Operational critique. An organizational critique is when a search team or agency does a critique on the team's response and the organizational strengths and weaknesses.

  o **Personal Critique** – Evaluate oneself regarding equipment, clothing, materials, etc., and their abilities and what can be improved or training or practice needed before the next callout.

An individual search team member has individual responsibilities to complete their process for going through the above components. The individual searcher must *preplan* to be prepared, receive *notification* to respond to a search, *check-in*, receives a *general briefing* from the plan section chief, then receives a *tactical briefing* from the operation section chief, conducts their search, completes a *debriefing* from the plan section chief, they may continue through several assignments before *check out* and then should conduct a *personal critique* of their performance.

General Briefing – this is a briefing conducted by the plan section chief and provides a general overview of the major aspects of the search mission, the incident action plan, and the situation past and present. This can be in form of a verbal briefing or it can be a situational status board with all the pertinent information about the search and the missing subject.

Tactical Briefing – this is a briefing conducted by the Operation Section Chief, or the crew leader and is specific to your tactical assignment and expectations. Most of the time this is conducted by someone in the operation section. In the absence of the Operation Section Chief the Incident Commander may conduct the Tactical Briefing.

When arriving on the scene, Check In at Staging and Sign-in on the ICS 211 sign in sheet. This will collect the pertinent information and will provide the necessary documentation regarding your participation in the incident. From here you will be tracked by Incident Command, Planning, Operations through Resource Status Unit (RESTAT) under Planning Section. This will ensure personnel accountability and allows command to manage resources.

> *"Do not repeat the tactics which have gained you one victory, but let your methods be regulated by the infinite variety of circumstances"*
> Sun Tzu

TACTICS

After determining where to search - ***Planning/Strategy***, the next phase is determining how to search - ***Tactics/Operations***. The process of determining how to search is based on objectives for the incident and the operational period.

Once the objectives have been determined, strategies to achieve the objectives are selected. Strategies lead to tactics employed to implement the strategy. Always remember that some type of response should occur immediately and this can be accomplished using Reflex Tasking.

Tactics are the core of the operations and are the methods used to carry out the plan strategies using the various types of available resources. The most basic search resource is a land search team using a map, a compass, and their senses, especially that of seeing and hearing.

A Land Search Team is made up of a minimum of 2 to 6 members. The functions of a land search team may include the following positions:
- ***Search team leader*** – leads the team based on the task objectives, based navigator input.
- ***Radio operator*** – handles all radio communications between the team and command.
- ***Navigator*** – understands the map, the task, and navigates the team using a compass, map, and GPS.
- ***Search team members*** – Searches using various search techniques using all of their senses. These may also be known as Flankers.

Additional information regarding the Team will be discussed in Chapter 10 – Search Teams. Teams going into the field should have some type of radio communications, map, compass, and maybe a GPS. Secondary or backup communications should be considered like a cell phone or another radio system like Amateur Radio.

The search team should be focused on searching for clues and the subject. There are thousands of clues and only one subject so the focus on clues will lead you to the subject. Clues can be investigated clues or physical clues within the search area. There are four types of clues - Physical, Recorded, Testimonial, and Analytical. Always remember, that the missing subject is a natural clue generator that will continually send or leave clues for searchers to find.

The searcher needs to focus on searching for clues for them to be clue aware. Clue awareness can be difficult with all the distractions of looking at the map, compass, GPS, and cell phone along with answering and talking on the radio and/or cell phone. Concentrating on looking (Searching) and listening is critical. Minimize distractions by delegating functions and duties amongst the team members. There are two broad categories of tactics which are **Passive** and **Active**. It is important to do passive techniques with the same level of effort as you would active techniques.

Two major strategies in search tactics are **Passive** (Indirect) and **Active** (Direct).

Passive Techniques strategies may involve:
- Confinement and Containment
- Attraction
- Investigation

The **Confinement** strategy involves the following tactics:
- Road/Trail Blocks
- String Lines/Signs
- Track Traps
- Perimeter Search

Confinement will keep the subject within the search area, detect if the subject has left the search area, or locate the subject on roads or trails.

Perimeter search can allow the trackers to cut sign on the boundaries where there are natural track traps determining if the subject crossed the boundaries such as fence lines, road edges, trails, streambeds, etc.

The **Attraction** strategy involves the following tactics:
- Lookouts
- Helicopter/Airplane Flyovers
- Public Address (PA) Sound Devices (Sirens)

Encourage the missing person to find the searchers (assumes the missing subject is mobile and conscious and has the ability to follow signals or directions to a safe place)

The **Investigation** strategy involves the following tactics:
- Completing the Missing Person Questionnaire
- Following up on leads or clues in determining the relevance
- Interviewing family, friends, neighbors, doctors, coworkers, and others

Obtaining missing person information and determining why the missing person went missing is critical before sending searchers into the field.

Pictorial of Confinement and Attraction Tactics:

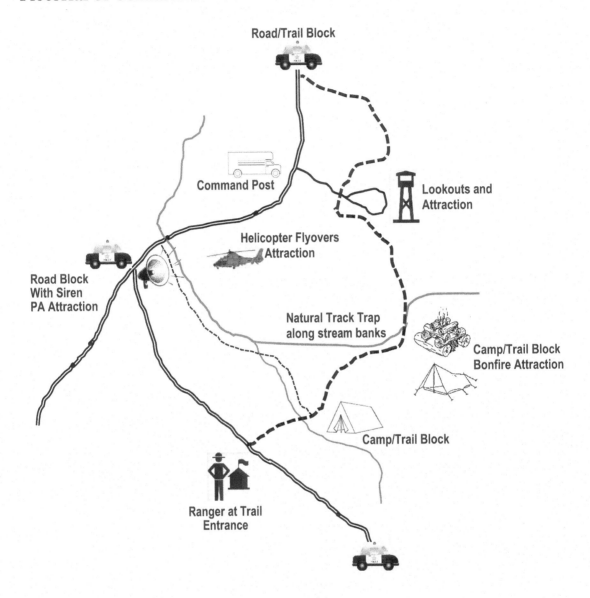

Search Planners and Search Team Members should understand Decision Points within a search area that could have caused the missing subject to become lost. **Decision Point** – The location at which a subject makes a choice between options of direction in which to head. The choice may not involve a conscious decision. *Lost Person Behavior – Robert J. Koester*

These are Points that the missing subject made a critical error in navigation. This can be a switchback or terrain feature intersection. Identifying these points earlier on helps with passive techniques placement of stationary trails or roadblocks or lookouts.

Active Search Tactics

Type I – hasty search
Type II – loose, area, sweep, or efficient search
Type III– tight, grade, evidence, or thorough search.

Criterion	Type I Speed	Type II Efficiency	Type III Thoroughness
Objective	Quickly search high probability areas and gain info on search areas.	Rapid search of large areas	Search with the absolute highest probability of detection (POD)
Definition	Fast initial response of well-trained, self-sufficient, and very mobile searchers that check areas most likely to produce clues or the subject the soonest.	Relatively fast, systematic search of high probability segments of the search area that produce high results per searcher-hour of effort.	Slow, highly systematic search using the most thorough techniques to provide the highest probability of detection possible.
Tactics	Linear Features Search (Trackline) Points of Interest (Spot)	Purposeful Wandering	
Considerations	Works best with responsive subject Offers immediate show of effort Helps define search area Clue consciousness is critical Planning is crucial for effective use Often determines where not to search	Often employed after hasty searchers, especially if clues were found. Best suited to responsive subjects. Often effective at finding clues. Between-searcher spacing is dependent on terrain and visibility.	Marking search segments is very important. Should be used only as a last resort. Very destructive to clues. Used when other methods of searching are unsuccessful.
Techniques	Investigation (personal physical effort) Check LKP & PLS for clues Follow known route Run trails and ridges Check area perimeter, confine the area Check hazards and attractions	Open grid line search with wide between-searcher spacing. Compass bearings or specific guides are often used to control search. Often applied to a defined area to follow-up a discovered clue. No overlap in area coverage Critical separation. Sound sweeps.	Closed grid or sweep search with small between-searcher spacing. Searched areas often overlap adjacent teams for better coverage.
Size of Team	Two or three very mobile, well-trained, self-sufficient searchers	May include three to seven skilled searchers, but usually just three.	Four to seven searchers, including both trained and untrained personnel.
Most Effective Resource	Investigators Trained hasty teams Human trackers Dogs Aircraft	Clue conscious search teams Human trackers and signcutters Dogs Aircraft	Trained grid search teams.

Type I Techniques - *Speed*

Checking the immediate area, trails, roads, buildings, campsites, and specific areas of high probability.
- Investigation
- Hasty Teams - 3 person teams
- Thorough checks of Last Know Location
- Following Known Routes
- Trail Running
- Perimeter / Proximity Check and search
- Sign Cutting/ Man-Tracking – expanding out from LKP or PLS
- Road Patrols
- Check Attractions
- Check Hazardous Areas
- Check Drainage's
- Ridge Running
- Bastard Search
- Locating any Clues
- ELT/PLB/Direction Finding Search
- Airscent Dog along the perimeter, road, trail, or drainage
- Bloodhound or trailing dog from Point Last Seen or Last Know Point

Linear Features Search (Trackline)
- Determine the most likely route subject would have gone and quickly cover this route.
- Often used for lost hikers, walkers;
- Conducted by initial responders;
- Need to specify the distance from the feature for desired coverage;
- Follows travel aids (trails, drainages, etc.);
- Navigation is the greatest challenge, start the task at a clear point;
- Downhill preferable;
- Clue awareness, especially at decision points, is critical; and
- Easily combined with sound and tracking techniques.

Points of Interest (Spot)
Thoroughly cover a specific area in which the subject may be located.
- Check Scenic overlooks, bathrooms, playgrounds, swim pools, bodies of water; and
- Check residence, outbuildings, and possible locations the missing subject may have visited.

All of these Type I Tactics should be applied before moving into Type II or Type III search tactics. Type I and Type II may overlap and can be accomplished without a lot of personnel.

Type II Techniques - *Efficiency*

Route (Area) Search

This tactic may require the search area to be segmented into searchable chunks of real estate.

Usually, the size of the segments should be no more than 100 acres with identifiable boundaries. Often, these boundaries are also likely routes the missing subject may have traveled, which may be natural or man-made. Topographical features are natural (ridges, streams, drainages, field edges) and manmade are roads, trails, fences, power or utility transmission line clearings.

Different types of resources can be applied to the area and may need to be researched multiple times.
- Airscent Dog
- 6 person Hasty Teams
- Open Grid Search
- Sound Sweep
- Critical Separation
  - Purposeful Wandering
  - 360-degree turn techniques
- Along a Ravine, Road, or Creek (Parallel Search)
- Helicopter search using FLIR or Day Camera (Record if possible)

A systematic search using several personnel in which search team members follow tracks parallel to a side boundary & maintain a predetermined separation.

- Search area may be covered in one or more passes;
- All searchers should attempt to walk in nearly straight lines parallel to the edge of the area, providing uniform, predictable coverage of the entire area;
- The baseline is usually formed along a search area boundary with searchers properly spaced apart;
  - Spacing will determine if the Tactic is less thorough or thorough
  - Spacing will be determined by the density of vegetation in the area
- Purposeful wandering may be employed;
- Team Leader keeps the team moving in the right direction, at a reasonable pace, and maintaining proper searcher separation.

Type III Techniques - *Thoroughness*

Large ground search teams with closed spacing search a defined area.

Area (Grid) Search
- Thorough tactic to raise POD and look for unresponsive subjects.
- Competent flankers required, if using emergent volunteers more experienced crew leaders required;
- The baseline is usually formed along a search area boundary with searchers properly spaced apart;
  - Spacing tight to ensure thorough tactical search
  - Spacing will be determined by the density of vegetation in the area
- Evidence type search may be shoulder to shoulder and conducted on hands and knees;
- The direction of the search follows a specific compass bearing;
- Purposeful wandering may be employed;
- Instead of large lines, used staggered starts and flagging tape; and
- Tight Grid Searching (thorough) is manpower intensive and should be considered as a last resort after other search tactics have been used and narrowed the search area down.

Other Techniques and Tactics

Proximity Search

Complete a Proximity Search of the LKP/PLS – No Longer than 10 Minutes
- Check the most likely areas
  - Beach, Bathhouses, concessions, bathrooms, visitor center, playgrounds, parking lots.
- Check the high probability areas
- Document in notes the various locations that were checked
- Ensure they are re-checked later

Sound Sweep

A method to search a relatively large area quickly using an attraction technique while searching. It requires that the missing person be responsive.
- Must be carefully coordinated, audible, and requires all to pause and listen for response;
- Sounds can often be heard even when the missing person cannot be seen; and
- Searchers will use whistles or call the missing subject's name at specific intervals.

Tracking

Is a technique that requires special training and lots of patience to first locate physical evidence of the subject's previous presence or passage through the area. The evidence may include footprints, bruised or broken vegetation, or far more subtle signs such as scuffs, flattening, color changes, or shine.

They can identify the print, size, and pattern of the shoe or footprint. They can measure the stride and may tell the subject's physical condition based on their walking behaviors.

Signcutting

Signcutting is the act of looking for sign or tracks to be able to establish a starting point for tracking.

When a physical clue has been located and it relates to our missing subject we can assume the clue did not fall out of the sky. The clue was brought in "entry route", left behind and the subject left "exit route". So signcutting is looking for tracks or sign and determining the direction of travel of the missing subject.

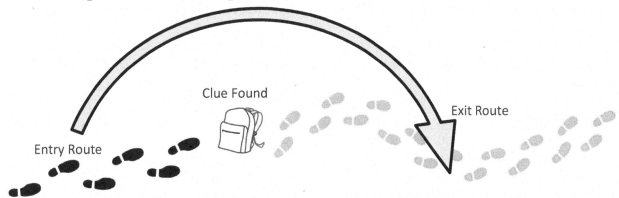

By conducting a 360 perimeter search around the found clue allows the tracker to identify the Entry and Exit Route and provides a direction of travel. This can also be accomplished with a scent discriminating dog using the found clue as to the scent article as long as the clue is verified to be the subjects.

Tracktraps

Natural "Track Traps" – are areas that tracks are easily seen in areas like embankments along streams, mudflats, fields of high grass, brushy thickets, or roadway edges, beaches, or soft soil areas.

Manmade "Track Traps" – are areas created by raking or plowing areas on trails or paths of least resistance. Cleared construction sites may be one.

Reflex Tasking - Initial tasks that follow standard scenario-based patterns and are sent into high Probability of Area (POA) areas during the start of the search. Once the first few resources arrive on the scene the incident commander can quickly send resources to the high probability areas based on the lost person behavior and the initial investigative information. Proximity Search would fall in this tasking type. Searching the house, up a trail from the PLS/LKP, going to the destination location, and checking the immediate area are all Reflex Tasking Activities.

Range Detection – Average Range of Detection (R_d) is a procedure that reasonably determines the searcher's detection capability. This assists in a more accurate way to determine effective sweep width (ESW). So, R_d is the average range of linear distance that a search object or clue is first detected when moving towards it in different directions. The ability to detect an object.

Night Time Searching

Different resources have advantages over others when searching at night. Environmental factors change and the behavior of the missing subject may also change as a result of the darkness. They tend to slow down and hunker down finding a place to lay down and rest giving searchers a tactical advantage to catching up.

Search Dogs especially airscent dogs work better at night due to the scent conditions.

Tracks show up better at night, early morning, and as dusk. The track at night shows up better when using a flashlight at a low angle and footprints do not dry up as quickly as in the day.

Voices travel further due to less ambient noise. Temperature differences allow the Thermal Imaging devices on aircraft and handheld to see well.

There are several disadvantages to searching at night. The field of view of the searchers is limited to the light source they bring and the darkness does not allow searchers to see everything near them which may cause them to miss clues and destroy clues or signs. Lights also hamper the searcher's night vision.

Nighttime searching is inherently more hazardous and difficult but that does not mean that a search should not be conducted. Using trained search teams who are used to searching at night should be considered.

Teams working together may use glow sticks on each other and on the search dog so that you can see and identify them in the dark. Glow sticks also do not affect night vision.

Route Search

Parallel Route Search :
Following adjacent to a Trail or Road.

Route Search :
Following a Trail, Road, Stream, or Linear Feature with Searches on either side.

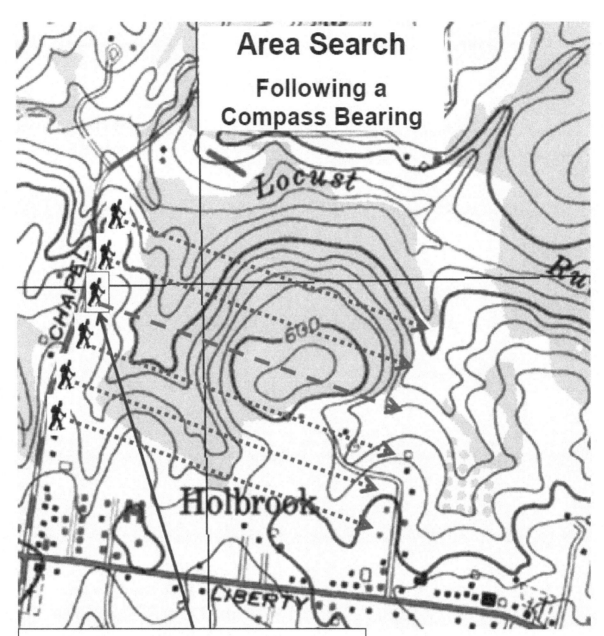

Area Search
Following a Compass Bearing

Compass Guide Person:
This search will follow a compass direction of 95 degrees (Magnetic) and other team member will guide off of them.

Route/Area Search

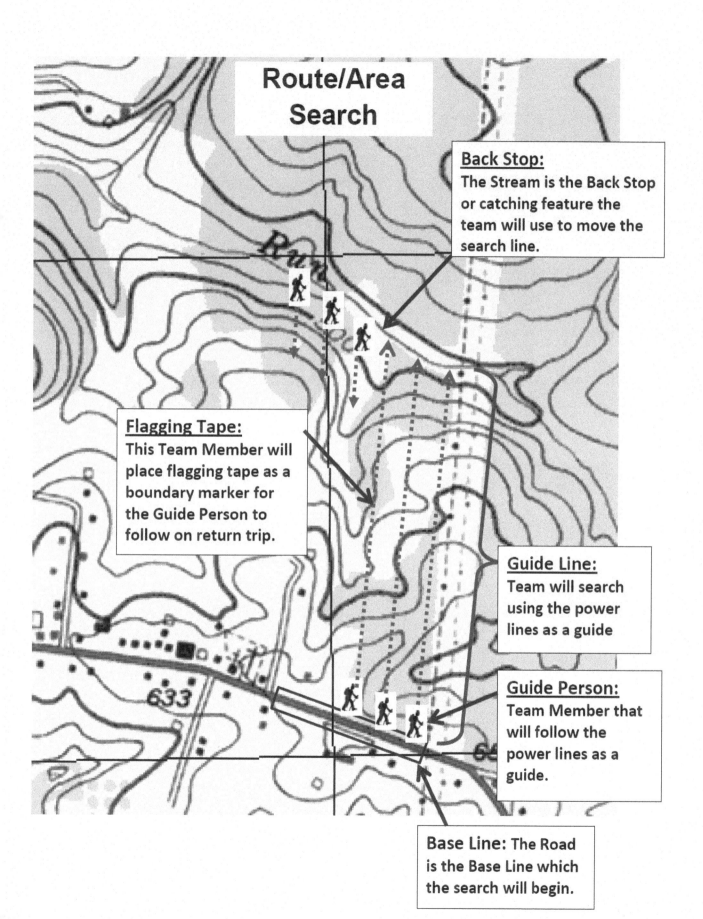

Back Stop:
The Stream is the Back Stop or catching feature the team will use to move the search line.

Flagging Tape:
This Team Member will place flagging tape as a boundary marker for the Guide Person to follow on return trip.

Guide Line:
Team will search using the power lines as a guide

Guide Person:
Team Member that will follow the power lines as a guide.

Base Line: The Road is the Base Line which the search will begin.

Chapter 10 – The Search Team Evaluation and Organizations

Objectives:

- The Student shall understand where to get information on finding a search and rescue team.
- The student shall be able to list various organizations that provide training, certifications, evaluations, and assistance to search teams and their members. *ASTM F3098 (16) – 4.1 – 4.11*
- The Student shall be able to identify and know the functions of a search team that will be deployed to the field.
- The student should be able to list some considerations a search team should consider when forming the search team organization.

Where to find a Team and Resources and the Training and Certification

Getting involved in search and rescue can be fun and exciting especially when you know that you are helping to save the life of another. Being on a search and rescue team is not easy. Some members train for years before ever responding to their first search and rescue incident or operations. The lives of the missing or lost subjects count on the quality and dedication of the teams who search for them. Most teams are looking for dedicated individuals that want to provide a quality service. Most team members dedicate a lot of hours, sacrifice a lot of personal time and money to get training to be able to serve on a search and rescue team. Most people find it very rewarding by giving back to their community, helping those that are in need, spending time in the outdoors, challenging yourself both physically and mentally, and spending time with like-minded people. Being part of a search and rescue team will take time and dedication to ensure your success on the team.

The best source of finding a search and rescue team is using the Internet. You have to decide what sorts of discipline you want to become involved in. Most people tend to get involved with a search dog team or an equine team so that they can spend time with their four-legged friends. In addition, contacting your local sheriff's department or law enforcement agency may be able to guide you to a search and rescue team.

Listed below are some organizations or agencies which may be able to also assist with finding a search and rescue team, equipment, training, certification, etc.:

National Association for Search and Rescue (NASAR)

The National Association for Search and Rescue, Inc., (NASAR) is a not-for-profit membership association dedicated to advancing professional, literary, and scientific knowledge in fields related to search and rescue. NASAR is comprised of thousands of paid and non-paid professionals interested in all aspects of search and rescue.

NASAR actively works toward the development of improved coordination and communications among federal, state, local, and volunteer groups. NASAR's primary goal is to develop and provide professional credentialing products and services for the search and rescue community.

Urban Search and Rescue Teams (USAR)

There are two types of USAR teams: there are State Urban Search and Rescue Teams organized at the state level and they are Federal Urban Search and Rescue Teams organized under the Federal Emergency Management Agency (FEMA). Most of the federal urban search and rescue teams are sponsored by a governmental organization. Most of these government organizations are fire and rescue departments and there are a few that are part of emergency management or law enforcement. Becoming part of this team is normally a collateral duty within a bigger organization such as a fire, rescue, or law enforcement organization. Considerations of becoming a member of this organization may require a member to become part of the fire or rescue system. This is also the same for most of the state search and rescue teams

Community Emergency Response Teams (CERT)

Some communities may have the Community Emergency Response Team (CERT) which is a program that educates volunteers about disaster preparedness for the hazards that may impact their area and trains them in the basic disaster response skills, such as fire safety, light search and rescue, team organization, and disaster medical operations. Some of these CERT organizations have trained members to do search and rescue within their community for those who go lost or missing.

Alzheimer's Association

The Alzheimer's Association is the leading voluntary health organization in Alzheimer's care, support, and research. The Alzheimer's Association provides support for those diagnosed with Alzheimer's disease with support services

One of the important services that the Alzheimer's Association offers is the MedicAlert + Safe Return program. The Association may have volunteers who put together posters of a potential missing dementia patient with Alzheimer's and post them within the community.

CAP – Civil Air Patrol

There are thousands of civil air patrol squadrons throughout the United States that are always looking for members. Those members can be trained and search and rescue providing both ground and air search capabilities. Under the resource chapter, we talked what are the capabilities of the Civil Air Patrol. They may be involved in day-to-day search and rescue operations as well as disaster response. We described Civil Air Patrol under Federal Resources in Chapter 1.

NCMEC - National Center for Missing and Exploited Children

The National Center for Missing and Exploited Children (NCMEC) looks to the public for avocation for children and their communities by sharing posters of missing children or disseminating safety tips to kids and families within the community. They also have a program called team hope which is a group of people who help others that have gone through the trauma of losing a child.

Team Adam - is a resource to law enforcement that provides on-site assistance to law enforcement agencies and families in a critical missing child case. Many retired law enforcement officers have become part of team Adam both as a volunteer and as a career. These individuals have significant law enforcement training and become consultants on a missing child case.

MRA - Mountain Rescue Association

The Mountain Rescue Association (MRA) is the oldest Search and Rescue association in the United States. With over 90 government authorized units in the US, Canada, and other countries, the MRA has grown to become the critical mountain search and rescue resource in the United States. The large majority of MRA membership is made up of unpaid professional volunteers who have been fully accredited in Mountain Search and Rescue operations.

The MRA focuses on teams in the credentialing of those teams. Individuals that want to volunteer in Mountain search and rescue can look at the MRA for a list of search and rescue teams within the area. Those teams will then outline their criteria for training, certification, and response.

CERT - Community Emergency Response Team - This program educates volunteers about disaster preparedness for the hazards that may impact their area and trains them in basic disaster response skills, such as fire safety, light search and rescue, team organization, and disaster medical operations.

Reserve Officers for Sheriff or Natural Resources

In a lot of the Western States, the Sheriff Offices has reserve deputies that provide search and rescue. Most Western States Sheriff's offices have the responsibility for search and rescue. To ensure the adequacy of their program they have reserve deputies which are volunteers that fall within the sheriff's structure and organization and provide search and rescue services.

There are various natural resource agencies in various states that have also a reserve officers' program that focuses on search and rescue.

Volunteer Search Teams

The majority of search and rescue in this country is provided by volunteers. Many of these volunteers are part of a nongovernmental organization that provides their services to the law enforcement agencies within a state. These volunteer search and rescue teams stand on their own providing their own insurance, equipment, resources, financial support, etc. to provide a service to their community.

Other Public Safety Resources

Fire and Rescue, Law Enforcement, and Emergency Management agencies are responsible for providing emergency response and may have their own search and rescue teams, search teams, rescue teams, etc. to support a missing person search. It is important to check with these agencies to see what type of capabilities they may have and who do they normally call for a search.

Emergent (Convergent) Volunteers and unaffiliated untrained Volunteers

Inherently on any search when there someone has gone missing the call for help will always bring out the *citizens without specialized training* but have a desire to help. They are referred to as emergent, convergent, or spontaneous volunteers. These individuals can be helpful at search incidents if managed and utilized properly.

In a community when an individual especially younger goes missing the news media will show emergent volunteers conducting a search known as grid search where they are lined up shoulder to shoulder screaming out the subject's name.

Most of the time these convergent volunteers have no personal protective clothing, survival equipment, or knowledge. They are usually not prepared for adverse weather conditions, long tasks, and the ability to search at night. There are many tasks in which emergent volunteers can help assist law enforcement. These tasks may include roadblocks, handing out flyers, door-to-door notification in urban environments, and providing logistical support and assistance.

Planning for the use of these individuals is critical. This can become logistically difficult to manage and takes away the focus of the searchers from doing their primary function. If these volunteers are going to be used it is suggested that the law enforcement agency conduct verification and identification along with performing a criminal check before allowing them to participate in the incident.

The function of State SAR Associations or Councils:

Most states Search and Rescue Associations or councils provide advocacy for the search and rescue teams. They will have relationships with state emergency management agencies, law enforcement agencies, and natural resources agencies that have the responsibility and jurisdiction for search and rescue. These associations and councils also ensure that standards are applied for personnel and teams to ensure that quality search operations are provided. They may use nationally recognized standards or standards developed by their own state standards that are approved by the state's responsible authority or Authority Having Jurisdiction (AHJ). Below is a list of some of the state associations and councils.

Listed Alphabetically
Alaska Search & Rescue Association
Appalachian Search & Rescue Conference
Arizona Search & Rescue Council
Arkansas State SAR Association
Bay Area Search & Rescue Council
Colorado Search & Rescue State Advisory Council
Florida Association for Search & Rescue
Idaho State Search & Rescue
Indiana Search & Rescue Association
Kentucky Search & Rescue
Maine Association for Search & Rescue
Maryland Search Teams Task Force
New Jersey Search & Rescue Council
New Mexico Search & Rescue Council
New York Federation of Search & Rescue Teams
North Carolina Search & Rescue Advisory Council
Oregon State Search & Rescue Advisory Committee
Pennsylvania Search & Rescue Council
Washington Search & Rescue Volunteer Advisory Council
West Virginia Search & Rescue Network
Wyoming Search & Rescue Council

Team Functions for a deployable team in the field:

The functions of a land search team positions:
- Search Team Leader
- Radio Operator
- Navigator
- Search Team Member
- Flanker

The Team Leader provides the overall direction for the search team in the field. All communications from the team to command and vice versa will be coordinated through the radio operator who will also be responsible for documentation utilizing the ICS 214. The navigator is responsible for knowing where the team is, reviewing the map, maintaining the coordinates, and operating the GPS to record the teams' tracks and the clues identified in the search area. Search team members have the responsibility of searching and focusing looking for clues and tracks. Typically, on a canine team, there are flankers. These are similar to search team members but are highly trained individuals that walk alongside the handler and the canines and can assist with navigation, communications, and searching. The K-9 handler is normally the search team leader.

Delegation of the responsibilities should be identified before leaving the command post to ensure that everybody understands their role and responsibilities.

Resource Identification and Evaluation

Resources should be evaluated based on six basic questions for their usefulness during a search operation. Resource should be identified in the Preplan. Tim Setnicka outlines in his book how to review resources.

"Meeting and greeting all of the resources in the preplan, while not a written requirement, is a fundamental task for the SAR Manager. A letter or phone call can substitute for a personal visit. Knowing who the other person or group is, what they can do, and how it operates often means the difference between successfully putting these resources into play or not."

Tim J. Setnicka Wilderness Search and Rescue 1980

1. **Availability**
   a. Are they ready to respond?
   b. Are there any special requesting procedures or conditions?

2. **Response Time**
   a. Type of response – Emergency or routine
   b. Staggered response
   c. Backup resources for the next operational period

3. **Capabilities**
   a. Are they ready for immediate deployment?
   b. Is this resource specialized, i.e., a K9 unit that is cadaver only?
   c. Are they capable to perform the task quickly, safely, and efficiently?

4. **Limitations**
   a. Special considerations – Radio, equipment, or food
   b. Competition – any ego issues
   c. Will they work with and for you?
   d. Are they in shape mentally and physically?
   e. How proficient or effective is the team
   f. Do they define their limitations or restrictions?

5. **Qualifications**
   a. Are they qualified?
   b. What standards does the team follow and apply to their members
   c. Do they have recommendations of past performance?
   d. What type of reoccurring training and certification do they apply?

6. **Back-Up**
   a. Do they work well with other teams and back each other up?
   b. What other teams or resources can they offer
   c. If they are not available, will they offer up another team or resource

A large number of SAR resources are volunteers. Most of these teams are non-governmental, non-profit organizations (NGOs). It is a best practice for the local authority having jurisdiction to vet these responders and maintain an up-to-date call-out list.

Requirements and considerations when forming a Search and Rescue Team

We have found that search and rescue teams are developed as a result of personal interests and the desire to help and as a result of one or more sorry incidents occurring within the community. They realized that there was a gap in training and capabilities and formed a search and rescue team. Some teams or individuals forming the team have not reached out or communicated with the local law enforcement agency or state law enforcement agencies and completed their homework.

Teams that do not fall within the emergency response system within the community or state may not get called unless they have developed a working relationship and agreements for a response. Some of these teams will freelance and expand their scope of operations to meet their personal needs versus the community needs. A member should always evaluate the team goals and objectives and ensure that it meets the criteria. Individuals and teams always have the inherent motivation to help others.

When considering forming a search and rescue team the first step that should be taken is to research if there is a SAR group in the area. Many states have created State Search and Rescue Councils, Associations, or Federations that are made up of search and rescue teams throughout that particular state.

Contact the responsible agency for search and rescue within your jurisdiction where the area in which you want to serve. Usually, this would be the Sheriff's Department or local law enforcement agency. There are emergency management agencies that may also be involved. Questions that should be sought are:

- Is there a sufficient need for a search and rescue team for this area? Without this, the program will not be sustainable.
- Established a working relationship
- determine that you will be called if trained.

Other Considerations
- Check the state's legal aspect of using volunteers in search and rescue.
- Determine how you will respond to a search call and who you would report to on most searches.

- Contact other search and rescue units in the area and assist in defining the team's role. This will establish good working relationships, concentrate specialties that are needed for the area.
- Develop a training plan. Before responding or going on any searches the unit should be fully trained and ready to respond. Not only do you jeopardize yourself in the subject, but you may give a bad impression of your unit causing it to not be called in the future even when you're fully trained.

Some government organizations will establish state standards and guidelines for search and rescue teams to follow especially when there are nine governmental search and rescue organizations.

Most of these organizations are law enforcement agencies that outline guidelines for teams to follow and to ensure they don't create a liability for them. They are used to augment their resources during the search.

There are times where the organization may have to apply via an application and provide the documentation to demonstrate and prove that they meet the established standards. Some of those standards will include the following:

- Possess and maintain a federal tax ID number and verification of the 501 (c) 3 nonprofit designation of the organization, or parent organization for deployable searchers.
- Provide proof and maintain various insurance coverages such as liability, accidental health, etc. on the organization deploying searchers. Liability coverage shall be at least $1 million of general liability coverages.
- Maintain a valid FCC license for search and rescue frequencies and all other license frequencies on which the unit may operate. Be able to produce individual searchers FCC licenses if they maintain an individual license.
- Be equipped with two-way radios capable of operating on the search and rescue frequencies for each deployable team member to include a base station.
- Be able to provide and maintain an active dispatch number and must be able to respond to search requests within 10 minutes regardless of the team's deployment status.
- Maintain written operational standards for field-deployable searchers, canines, and or equestrian.
- Maintain and adhere to written policies of the organization governing search response, member conduct, record-keeping, due process, and confidentiality.

- Maintain written training and evaluation records for each deployable searcher, canine, and/or equestrian.
- Maintain a list of unit equipment, logistics, and capabilities
- to provide an internal process for initial testing, and retesting every three years or less for each deployable team member in each individual's search discipline.
- Each member of the team should have a team picture ID card that identifies the member as being part of the organization.
- Organizations shall have a policy for the organization and its members to refrain from posting or sharing mission information on social media outlets.
- The organization will provide detailed criteria for the standards, certification, and recertification for each of their team members and what equipment is required by that team member.

References

Alzheimer's Association. Safe Return®.
http://www.alz.org/we_can_help_safe_return.asp

Bannerman, C., Foster, S., & Wade, M. (1999). **Introduction To Search And Rescue**. Chantilly, VA: National Association for Search and Rescue

Cooper, Donald C., Patrick (Rick) LaValla, and Robert (Skip) Stoffel. 1999. **Search And Rescue Fundamentals**: Basic skills and knowledge to perform wilderness, inland, search and rescue, 3rd ed., revised. Tacoma, WA: ERI International.

Cooper, D. C. (Ed.) 2005. **Fundamentals of Search and Rescue**. Jones and Bartlett Pubs. Sundbury, Massachusetts, 01776 U.S.A. and Nat. Assoc, for Search and Rescue, Centreville, Virginia, 20120-2020.

Hill, Kenneth A. **Lost Person Behavior**. 1997. Ottawa: National SAR Secretariat.

Hill, Kenneth A. **Managing the Lost Person Incidents**. 2nd Ed., 2007 Chantilly, VA: National Association for Search and Rescue.

Kelley, Dennis. **Mountain Search for the Lost Victim**. California. 3rd Printing 1987.

KOESTER, R. J. 2008. **Lost Person Behavior: A Search and Rescue Guide on Where to Look – for Land, Air and Water.** dbs Productions LLC, Charlottesville, Virginia, 22903, U.S.A. 396p. ISBN 978-1-879471-39-9

LaValle, P. (1999). **Search is an Emergency: Field Coordinator's Handbook for Managing Search Operations** (3rd Ed.). Olympia, WA: ERI International, Inc.

Martin, E. H., Elinsky, J., & Hourihan, D. (2008). **Introduction To Search And Rescue**. Chantilly, VA: National Association for Search and Rescue.

NASAR, **Incident Commander Field Handbook: Search and Rescue**. National Association for Search and Rescue, 1987.

National Wildfire Coordinating Group (NWCG). **The Incident Command System**, National Training Curriculum, Developed by the Interagency Steering Group. Boise, ID: National Interagency Fire Center, Division of Training 1994.

National Search and Rescue Committee [NSARC]. (2000). **United States National Search and Rescue Supplement to the International Aeronautical and Maritime Search and Rescue Manual.** Washington, DC: NSARC

National Search and Rescue Committee [NSARC]. (2011). **Land Search and Rescue Addendum** - Land Search and Rescue Addendum To The National Search And Rescue Supplement To The International Aeronautical And Maritime Search And Rescue Manual. Washington, DC: NSARC, dbs Production (2012)

Setnicka, Tim. **Wilderness Search and Rescue.** K. Andrasko, Ed. Boston MA: Appalachian Mountain Club, 1980.

STOFFEL, R. C. 2005. (2nd Ed.) **The Handbook for Managing Land Search Operations**. ERI Publications & Training. Cashmere. Washington 98815 U.S.A. 424p. ISBN 0-9709583-2-3.

Syrotuck, W.G. (1977). **Analysis of Lost Person Behavior**: An Aid to Search Planning. Canastota, YN: Arner Publications, Inc.

Taylor, Albert (Ab) and Donald Cooper. **Fundamentals of Mantracking**: The Step-By-Step Method. 2nd Ed., Olympia, WA: Emergency Response Institute and National Rescue Consultants, 1997.

Young, Christopher and John Wehbring. 2007. Urban Search: **Managing Missing Person Searches in the Urban Environment.** Virginia: dbS Production 2007.

Glossary of Search and Rescue Terms

Average Maximum Detection Range (AMDR)	Is the distance on average that a sensor (searcher) has the maximum detection range (Rd) to detect (see) an object in specific environmental conditions as well as vegetation or any ground cover or other obstacles in their search segment.
Area Effectively Swept (Z)	A measure of the area that can be (or was) effectively searched by searchers within the limits of search speed, endurance, and effective sweep width. The area effectively swept (Z) equals the effective sweep width (W) times search speed (V) times hours spent in the search area (T). That is, Z = (W x V) x T for one searcher or one resource (such as a ground searcher, dog team, boat, or aircraft and its crew).
Attraction Strategies	Is a passive search technique that attracts or encourages the missing person to come to the searchers that are conducting attraction activities. (Calling for or Whistling for the Subject, Lookout posts, helicopter or airplane flyovers, or anything that will grab the attention of the missing subject and attract them to a searcher.
Clue Awareness	Is the searchers ability to detect a clue based on their knowledge, training, and exerience. They can make a determination of the relationship of an object found to the missing subject and the search. Have an understanding how to find clues at various times of the day and at night and how to handle and process the clue. Understand the categories of a clue.
Coverage (C)	The ratio of the area effectively swept (Z) to the area searched (A), that is, C = Z/A. Coverage may be thought of as a measure of "thoroughness." The probability of detection (POD) of a search is determined by the coverage
Critique	A thorough review of an operations reviewing the positives and negatives and determining the effectiveness and weaknesses of the preplan and developing action items to improve the preplan and determine future training, equipment needs, and processes for the next incident.
Decision Points	The location at which a subject makes a choice between options of direction in which to head. The choice may not involve a conscious decision. Lost Person Behavior – Robert J. Koester
Demobilization	Is the process of returning all equipment, materials, and personnel back to their original ready status, replacing and restoring all used equipment and materials, and ensuring the safe return of all personnel. It is also the process of releasing resources from the incident.
Detection Range or Range of Detection (Rd)	The average of linear distances at which a search object is first detected when moving toward it from multiple angles.
Effective Sweep Width (W)	A measure of the effectiveness with which a particular sensor can detect a particular object under specific environmental conditions; a measure of detectability. Effective sweep width depends on the search object, the sensor, and the environmental conditions prevailing at the time and place of the search. There is no simple or intuitive definition, although it is possible to illustrate the concept.
Efficient Search	Relatively fast, systematic search of high probability segments of the search area that produces high results per searcher hour of effort and is a rapid search of large areas. Criterion is Efficiency.
Effort (z or TLL) - a.k.a., Track Line Length.	The total distance traveled by all searchers (or a boat or aircraft and its crew) while searching in the assigned segment. Loosely speaking, the number of searcher-hours expended while searching can be called "effort," but without knowing the average search speed, it cannot be used to compute coverage.

Glossary of Search and Rescue Terms

General Briefing	This is a briefing conducted by the plans section chief and provides a general overview of the major aspects search mission, the incident action plan, and the situation past and present.
Hasty Search	is a fast initial response of well trained, self sufficient, and very mobile searchers that check/search areas most likely to produce clues or the subject the soonest. The Criterion is Speed.
Incident Command System (ICS)	is a standardized, on scene, all hazard incident management concept and based upon a flexible, scalable response organization providing a common framework within which people can work together effectively on an emergency scene.
Initial Planning Point (IPP)	It is a point or base datum point, that never changes and where all search planning is based on. It may be the Point Last Seen (PLS) or the Last Known Point (LKP). It may also be appoint entirely separate based on the best available investigative information.
Last Known Point (LKP)	It is the last substantiated position based on clues or evidence belonging to the missing subject and indicating that the missing subject was known to be.
Limited Continuous Search	It is when the mission is suspended but not the search. The search continues on a limited basis while the investigation continues as an open missing person case. The limited search will post signs, inform the public and media, use the area for search training areas, and hold searches periodically in the area to undercover any new clues.
Misplaced Person	is a person who is aware of their location, has the ability to return to a place of safety and their life is not endangered or in peril, but they are simply misplaced or delayed.
Mission	Is an operation conducted by using various type of resources both management and field personnel to find a missing or lost person.
Mission Suspension	It is when the search mission has been suspended due to weather issues, lack of clues or information, or lack of resources and the subject has not been located. The mission may be suspended due to information the subject is not in the area. It may be suspended after a significant search effort but yields not clues and continues as a Limited Continuous Search.
Mission Termination	It is when the missing subject has been located and rescuedor recovered and the investigation is concluded and all resources have been demobilized.
Negilence - Mal Intent	Conduct which is malicious, willful, wanton.
Negligence (Fault)	An act which a reasonable and prudent person would not have under taken, failure to act within the standard of care or render aid when a duty exists, and harm or injury or damage occurred as a violation of an established standard of care.
Negligence - Gross Negligence	Great Departure from the Standard of Care
Negligence Per Se	An act or omission has been done in violation of a statute or regulation which results in harm to persons or property.
Planning Data	Information about the missing subject and used for developing strategies and focuses on past and present events leading up to the subject going missing, lost person behavior, weather, personality traits, medical and physical capabilities, and detectability and survivability.
PMA - Positive Mental Attitude	PMA implies that one has a vision of good natured change in one's mind; it employs a state of mind that continues to seek, find and execute ways to win, or find a positive outcome, regardless of the circumstances.

Glossary of Search and Rescue Terms

Point Last Seen (PLS)	It is the point where the subject was last seen by a witness, family member, or caught on video at a specific time and location.
Preplanning	It is a process which reviews the vulnerabilities of a community regarding a future emergency situation like missing persons and develops a plan of action that will be followed as a guide to ensure and effective operations.
Probability of Area (POA)	(also, Probability of Containment [POC]). The probability that the search object is contained within the boundaries of a region, segment, or other geographic area.
Probability of Detection (POD)	The probability of the search object being detected, assuming it was in the segment searched. POD measures sensor effectiveness, thoroughness, and quality. POD is a function of the coverage (C) achieved in the segment
Probability of Success (POS)	The probability of finding the search object with a particular search. pas measures search effectiveness. The accumulated probability of finding the search object with all the search effort expended over all searches to date is called "cumulative pas" (POScum).
Range of Detection (*Rd*)	Range of Detection is the average range of linear distance that a search object or clue is first detected when moving towards it at different directions.
Range of Extinction (*Re*)	The average of linear distances at which a search object is no longer seen after it has been detected while moving away from it from multiple angles.
Recklessness	A deliberate act or omission, counter to the Standard of Care completed with knowledge of the standard
Recovery	Is the location and evacuation of a body of a fatality.
Reflex Tasking	Initial tasks that follow standard scenario-based patterns and are sent into high Probability of Area (POA) areas during the start of the search.
Region	A subset of the search area based only on factors that affect POA; that is, regions may require segmentation prior to searching. Regions are based on probability of the search object's location, not on suitability for assigning search resources. A region may contain searchable segments, or a region itself may be a searchable segment. A searchable segment may also contain one or more regions (based on probability), but rarely are the available data good enough to distinguish such small regions in ground search situations.
Rescue	To access, stabilize and evacuate distressed or injured persons by whatever means necessary to ensure their timely transfer to an appropriate care facility or to a familiar environment.
Responsible Authority	Is the government agency or agencies who have legal responsibility for finding missing persons and has jurisdiction over the area where the person becomes missing. Due to the potential criminal nature of missing persons Search and Rescue operations the responsible authority is the Law Enforcement Agency of that jurisdiction.
SAR Emergency	Is a search and rescue incident that requires the utilization of resources to resolve the emergency, due to a threat or potential threat to life or property.
Search	Is to identify and locate persons or person who are or may become distressed or injured and are unable to return to a place of safety on their own.
Search and Rescue	Is the employment of available personnel, facilities, and resources in rendering aid to persons and property in distress, or potential distress, in the air, water, and on the land. It is any operation aimed at helping someone who cannot solve his or her problem alone. The problem may or may not involve an injury, but if no one acts, an injury could result (thirst, starvation, or hypothermia) in death.

Glossary of Search and Rescue Terms

Search Area	The area determined by the search planner, which is to be searched by SAR personnel to look for a search object. The search area includes the smallest area, consistent with all available information, which contains all of the possible search object locations, and therefore includes all regions and segments. The search area may be divided into regions based on the probable scenarios and into segments for the purpose of assigning specific tasks to the available search resources.
Search Object	A ship, aircraft, or other craft missing or in distress, or survivors, or related search objects, persons, or evidence for which a search is being conducted. A generic term used to indicate the lost person or evidence (clue) related to a lost subject. In the same segment, different search objects generally have different effective sweep widths (or "detectabilities"). This means that for any given search of a segment, different coverage areas, and hence different POD values, will be achieved for different search objects. A live, human search object is often referred to as a search subject.
Search Speed (V)	The average rate of travel (speed over the ground) of searchers while engaged in search operations within a segment.
Searching Data	Information that the searcher would need to be aware of to effectively locate and identify and call for the missing subject. Such information is name to call, clothing and physical description, items carried, shoe print description and etc.
Sector/Segment	A designated subarea (subset of the search area) to be searched by one or more specifically assigned search resources. The search planner determines the size of a segment. The boundaries of a segment are identifiable both in the field and on a map, and are based on suitability for assigning search resources, not probability of the search object's location.
Sensor	Human senses (sight, hearing, touch, etc.), those of specially trained animals (such as dogs), or electronic devices used to detect the object of a search. A human, multi-sensor platform is often referred to as a "searcher."
Sign Cutting	is the act of looking for sign in order to determine a starting point from which to begin tracking. Trackers when cutting sign will search perpendicular to the suspected path of the missing subject.
Single Resource	Single Resources may be individuals, a piece of equipment and its personnel complement or a crew or team of individuals with an identified supervisor.
Strategy	describes a broad perspective on how resources are to be used to achieve some goal. It will outline the desired objective to be accomplished. Strategy constitutes an overall plan of action.
Strike Team	Strike Teams are a set number of resources of the same kind and type with common communications operating under the direct supervision of a Strike Team Leader.
Tactic	Is the resources being deployed to the field and conduct a search tactic to meet the defined strategy or objective. Tactics are the techniques, procedures & methods used to find a missing person.
Tactical Briefing	This is a briefing conducted by the incident commander, operations sections chief, or crew leader and is specific to your tactical assignment and expectations.
Task Force	Task Forces are a combination of mixed resources with common communications operating under the direct supervision of a Task Force Leader.
Thorough Search	Is slow, highly systematic search using the most thorough techniques to provide the highest probability of detection possible and is used as last resort and criterion is thoroughness.

Search and Rescue Acronyms

AFRCC   Air Force Rescue Coordination Center

CAP   Civil Air Patrol

CERT   Community Emergency Response Team

FEMA   Federal Emergency Management Agency

FLIR   Forward Looking Infra-Red

ICP   Incident Command Post

ICS   Incident Command System

IC   Incident Commander

IPP   Initial Planning Point

LKP   Last Known Point

LPQ   Lost Person Questionnaire

NASAR   National Association for Search and Rescue

NIMS   National Incident Management System

NRF   National Response Framework

PLS   Point Last Seen

POA   Probability of Area

POD   Probability of Detection

POS   Probability of Success

PIO   Public Information Officer

SAR   Search and Rescue

USAF   United States Air Force

USCG   United States Coast Guard

USNG   United States National Grid

UTM   Universal Transverse Mercator

Anatomy of a SAR Incident

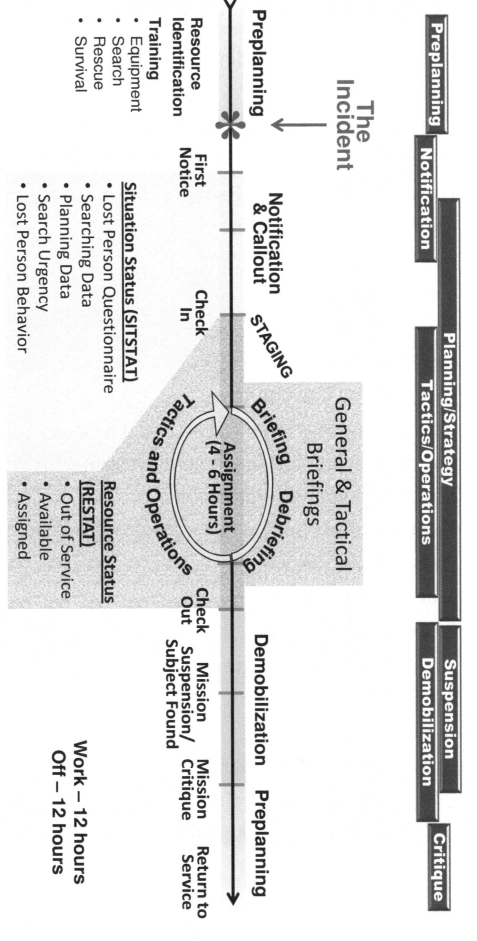

Preplanning

Notification

Planning/Strategy
Tactics/Operations

Suspension
Demobilization

Critique

The Incident

Preplanning

Resource Identification

Training
- Equipment
- Search
- Rescue
- Survival

First Notice

Notification & Callout

Situation Status (SITSTAT)
- Lost Person Questionnaire
- Searching Data
- Planning Data
- Search Urgency
- Lost Person Behavior

Check In

STAGING

General & Tactical Briefings

Tactics and Operations

Briefing — Debriefing

Assignment (4 - 6 Hours)

Resource Status (RESTAT)
- Out of Service
- Available
- Assigned

Check Out

Demobilization Preplanning

Mission Suspension/ Subject Found

Mission Critique

Return to Service

Work – 12 hours
Off – 12 hours

Briefings

General – Overall – given by Planning Section Chief
Tactical – Specific Task – given by Operation Section Chief

Designed by: Cole Brown©

Date: _____
Time: _____

SEARCH URGENCY FORM

Remember that the lower the number the more urgent the response

A. NUMBER OF SUBJECTS
1 Person --- 1
2 People --- 2
3 or more -- 3

B. AGE
Very young -- 1
Other -- 2-4
Very old -- 1

C. MEDICAL CONDITION
Known illness requiring medication ---------------------------------- 1
Suspected illness or injury --- 2
Healthy --- 3
Known fatality -- 4
Potential vision impairment --- 1

D. PHYSICAL CONDITION
Unfit --- 1
Fit --- 2
Very fit -- 3

SUBJECT PROFILE: Subtotal _____

E. CLOTHING PROFILE
Inadequate or insufficient-- 1
Adequate-- 2
Very good -- 3

F. EQUIPMENT PROFILE
Inadquate for activity / environment--------------------------------- 1
Questionable --- 2
Adequate-- 3
Very well equipped --- 4

G. EXPERIENCE PROFILE
Not experienced, not familiar with the area ------------------------- 1
Not experienced, knows the area ------------------------------------- 2
Experienced, not familiar with area --------------------------------- 3
Experienced, knows the area --- 4

H. WEATHER PROFILE
Existing hazardous weather -- 1
Hazardous forecast*(8 hours or less)* -------------------------------- 2
Hazardous forecast*(more than 8 hours)* ------------------------------ 3
No hazardous weather forecast --------------------------------------- 4

I. TERRAIN AND HAZARDOUS PROFILE
Known hazards -- 1
Difficult terrain--- 2
Few hazards -- 3
Easy terrain, no known hazards -------------------------------------- 4

If any of the nine categories are rated as one(1), regardless of the total, the search may require an immediate response.

TOTAL _____

9-17	18-27	28-33
URGENT RESPONSE	**MEASURED RESPONSE**	**EVALUATE AND INVESTIGATE**

The total should range between 9 and 33 with 9 indicating the greatest urgency.

PLANNING AND SEARCHING DATA

PLANNING DATA - Information needed for adequate search planning strategy.

A. Category of the Subject
    1.detectability of the subject
    2.survivability of the subject

B. Point last seen
    1.be as accurate as possible
    2.list specifics of person reporting the incident

C.Circumstances of Loss
    1.Exactly when and where was the subject missing?
    2.Missing from known location, enroute, in wilderness.
    3.Exactly how long has the subject been missing.

D.Subject's Trip Preparation
    1.Equipment necessary for survivability/tracking/clues.
    2.Experience

E.Physical Condition of the Subject
    1.Before the time of loss.
    2.At the time of loss.

F.Medical condition
    1.Any medication/illness/injury

G.Personality Traits of the Subject
    1.Is the subject expressive,smart,assertive,logical,etc.

H.Weather
    1.At time of loss.
    2.Predicted during mission.

I.Terrain Analysis
    1.Terrain type.
    2.Possible routes.
    3.points of attraction/confusion.

SEARCHING DATA
    1. Name to call
    2. Physical description
    3. Clothing worn, types, brands, colors
    4. Shoe print description
    5. Equipment Description(particularly discardable items)
    6. Brands of cigarettes, gum, candy, other

Planning and searching data is needed in order to:
    1. Establish priorities and urgency.
    2. Look for clues.
    3. Apply initial searchers to the field.
    4. apply initial search tactics.

Incident Command System (ICS)

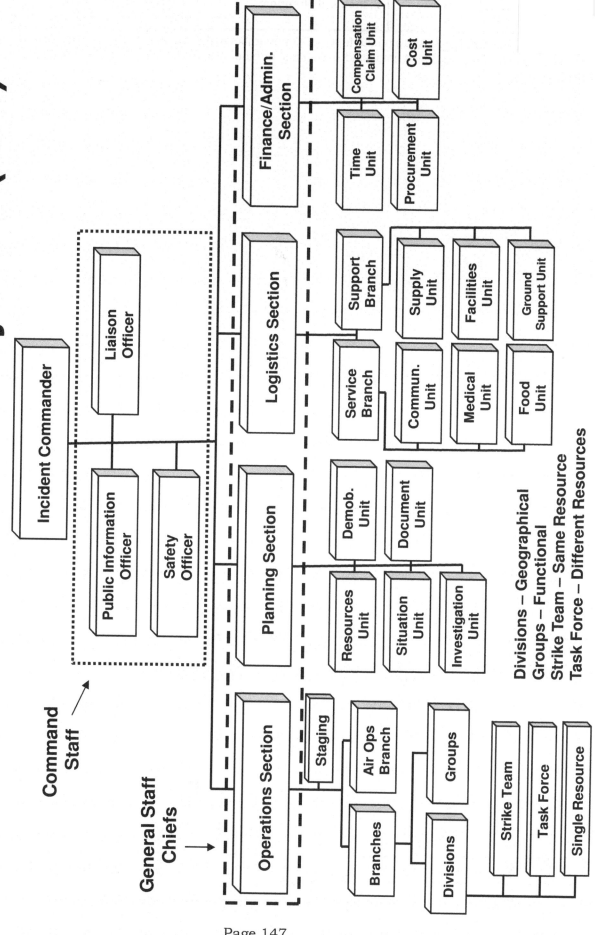

Command Staff

General Staff Chiefs

Incident Commander

Liaison Officer

Public Information Officer

Safety Officer

Operations Section

Planning Section

Logistics Section

Finance/Admin. Section

Staging

Air Ops Branch

Branches

Divisions

Groups

Strike Team

Task Force

Single Resource

Resources Unit

Situation Unit

Investigation Unit

Demob. Unit

Document Unit

Service Branch

Support Branch

Commun. Unit

Medical Unit

Food Unit

Supply Unit

Facilities Unit

Ground Support Unit

Time Unit

Procurement Unit

Compensation Claim Unit

Cost Unit

Divisions – Geographical
Groups – Functional
Strike Team – Same Resource
Task Force – Different Resources

INCIDENT BRIEFING (ICS 201)

1. Incident Name:	2. Incident Number:	3. Date/Time Initiated: Date: Time:

4. Map/Sketch (include sketch, showing the total area of operations, the incident site/area, impacted and threatened areas, overflight results, trajectories, impacted shorelines, or other graphics depicting situational status and resource assignment):

5. Situation Summary and Health and Safety Briefing (for briefings or transfer of command): Recognize potential incident Health and Safety Hazards and develop necessary measures (remove hazard, provide personal protective equipment, warn people of the hazard) to protect responders from those hazards.

6. Prepared by: Name: _____ Position/Title: _____ Signature: _____

ICS 201, Page 1	Date/Time: _____

INCIDENT BRIEFING (ICS 201)

1. Incident Name:	2. Incident Number:	3. Date/Time Initiated: Date: Time:

7. Current and Planned Objectives:

8. Current and Planned Actions, Strategies, and Tactics:

Time:	Actions:

6. Prepared by: Name: _____ Position/Title: _____ Signature: _____

ICS 201, Page 2 | Date/Time: _____

INCIDENT BRIEFING (ICS 201)

1. Incident Name:	2. Incident Number:	3. Date/Time Initiated: Date: Time:

9. Current Organization (fill in additional organization as appropriate):

```
                              ┌──────────────────────┐      ┌──────────────────────┐
                              │ Incident Commander(s) │──────│   Liaison Officer    │
                              │                       │      └──────────────────────┘
                              │                       │      ┌──────────────────────┐
                              │                       │──────│    Safety Officer    │
                              │                       │      └──────────────────────┘
                              │                       │      ┌──────────────────────┐
                              │                       │──────│ Public Information Officer │
                              └──────────────────────┘      └──────────────────────┘

   ┌──────────────────┐   ┌──────────────────┐   ┌──────────────────┐   ┌──────────────────┐
   │ Planning Section │   │ Operations       │   │ Finance/Admin.   │   │ Logistics        │
   │ Chief            │   │ Section Chief    │   │ Section Chief    │   │ Section Chief    │
   └──────────────────┘   └──────────────────┘   └──────────────────┘   └──────────────────┘
```

6. **Prepared by:** Name: _____	Position/Title: _____	Signature: _____
ICS 201, Page 3	Date/Time: _____	

INCIDENT BRIEFING (ICS 201)

1. Incident Name:	2. Incident Number:	3. Date/Time Initiated: Date: Time:

10. Resource Summary:

Resource	Resource Identifier	Date/Time Ordered	ETA	Arrived	Notes (location/assignment/status)
				☐	
				☐	
				☐	
				☐	
				☐	
				☐	
				☐	
				☐	
				☐	
				☐	
				☐	
				☐	
				☐	
				☐	
				☐	
				☐	

6. Prepared by: Name: _____ Position/Title: _____ Signature: _____

ICS 201, Page 4   Date/Time: _____

INCIDENT OBJECTIVES

	1. INCIDENT NAME	2. DATE PREPARED	3. TIME PREPARED

4. OPERATIONAL PERIOD (DATE/TIME)

5. GENERAL CONTROL OBJECTIVES FOR THE INCIDENT (INCLUDE ALTERNATIVES)

6. WEATHER FORECAST FOR OPERATIONAL PERIOD

7. GENERAL SAFETY MESSAGE

8. ATTACHMENTS (✔ IF ATTACHED)

- ☐ ORGANIZATION LIST (ICS 203)
- ☐ ASSIGNMENT LIST (ICS 204)
- ☐ COMMUNICATIONS PLAN (ICS 205)

- ☐ MEDICAL PLAN (ICS 206)
- ☐ INCIDENT MAP
- ☐ TRAFFIC PLAN

- ☐ _____
- ☐ _____
- ☐ _____

9. PREPARED BY (PLANNING SECTION CHIEF)

10. APPROVED BY (INCIDENT COMMANDER)

202 ICS (1/99)

NFES 132

ORGANIZATION ASSIGNMENT LIST (ICS 203)

1. Incident Name:		2. Operational Period: Date From:	Date To:
		Time From:	Time To:

3. Incident Commander(s) and Command Staff:		7. Operations Section:		
IC/UCs		Chief		
		Deputy		
Deputy		Staging Area		
Safety Officer		**Branch**		
Public Info. Officer		Branch Director		
Liaison Officer		Deputy		
4. Agency/Organization Representatives:		Division/Group		
Agency/Organization	Name	Division/Group		
		Division/Group		
		Division/Group		
		Division/Group		
		Branch		
		Branch Director		
		Deputy		
5. Planning Section:		Division/Group		
Chief		Division/Group		
Deputy		Division/Group		
Resources Unit		Division/Group		
Situation Unit		Division/Group		
Documentation Unit		**Branch**		
Demobilization Unit		Branch Director		
Technical Specialists		Deputy		
		Division/Group		
		Division/Group		
		Division/Group		
6. Logistics Section:		Division/Group		
Chief		Division/Group		
Deputy		**Air Operations Branch**		
Support Branch		Air Ops Branch Dir.		
Director				
Supply Unit				
Facilities Unit		**8. Finance/Administration Section:**		
Ground Support Unit		Chief		
Service Branch		Deputy		
Director		Time Unit		
Communications Unit		Procurement Unit		
Medical Unit		Comp/Claims Unit		
Food Unit		Cost Unit		

9. Prepared by: Name: _____ Position/Title: _____ Signature: _____

ICS 203	**IAP Page** _____	Date/Time: _____

ASSIGNMENT LIST (ICS 204)

1. Incident Name:	2. Operational Period: Date From: Date To: Time From: Time To:	3. Branch:
4. Operations Personnel: <u>Name</u> <u>Contact Number(s)</u> Operations Section Chief: _____ Branch Director: _____ Division/Group Supervisor: _____		**Division:** **Group:** **Staging Area:**

5. Resources Assigned:

Resource Identifier	Leader	# of Persons	Contact (e.g., phone, pager, radio frequency, etc.)	Reporting Location, Special Equipment and Supplies, Remarks, Notes, Information

6. Work Assignments:

7. Special Instructions:

8. Communications (radio and/or phone contact numbers needed for this assignment):

<u>Name/Function</u>   <u>Primary Contact: indicate cell, pager, or radio (frequency/system/channel)</u>

_____ / _____   _____

_____ / _____   _____

_____ / _____   _____

_____ / _____   _____

9. Prepared by: Name: _____ Position/Title: _____ Signature: _____

| ICS 204 | IAP Page _____ | Date/Time: _____ |

TASK ASSIGNMENT FORM

TYPE OF TASK: ❑ Tracking/Trailing ❑ Airscent ❑ Hasty ❑ Confinement ❑ Visual Tracker TASK COMPLETE: ❑ Yes ❑ No
❑ Helicopter ❑ Investigation ❑ Ground Area ❑ Other: _____

DATE:	TASK NO. [Day –Task #]	TEAM IDENTIFIER	TYPE OF TEAM	TIME OUT	DISPATCHER

ASSIGNMENT

OPERATIONAL PERIOD	TASK MAP/QUADRANGLE	MAP DATUM: ❑ NAD83 ❑ NAD27 ❑		USNG/UTM 100,000 Meter Grid: ❑ 17S ❑18S

EXPECTED TIME TO SEARCH:	SIZE OF SEARCH TASK AREA: ❑ Acres: _____ ❑Sq. KM _____	TYPE OF TACTIC: ❑ Hasty ❑ Efficient ❑ Thorough	TYPE OF SEARCH: ❑ Area ❑ Linear

TASK INSTRUCTIONS:

TRANSPORTATION INSTRUCTIONS ❑ Own Vehicle ❑ Walk ❑ Other: _____	EQUIPMENT REQUIREMENTS ❑ 24-hour Pack ❑ Radio ❑ Medical/Rescue ❑ GPS ❑ Other: _____

PERSONNEL

Team Leader:		K9 Member:	
Team Member:			

COMMUNICATIONS

TEAM CALL SIGN/ID:	PRIMARY FREQ. ❑ 155.160 ❑ 155.205 ❑ 155.235 ❑ _____	SECONDARY FREQ. ❑ 155.160 ❑155.205 ❑ 155.235 ❑ _____	Other:

TEAM LEADERS CELL PHONE #:	COMMAND POST #:	Other Numbers:

INSTRUCTIONS:

ADDITIONAL COMMENTS

DEBRIEFING CHECKLIST
To be completed by Search Management

Time task completed: _____   Name of Debriefer: _____

Date / Time prepared: _____   Total Time actually searching: _____

Time Searching Started: _____   Time Searching Stopped:_____

How Many Searchers on Team: _____   How far apart was spacing: _____ (Ft.)

The Size of the Seach Area **Searched**: _____ (Acres) _____ (Sq. Kilometers)

TEAM PERFORMANCE:

Visibility / weather conditions: _____

Terrain conditions: _____ Hazards noted: _____

Was task completed as assigned? YES NO *IF NO, explain*:_____
_____

Average Maximum Detection Range (AMDR) _____(Ft.) Total Track Line Length (TLL): ___ (Ft.)

Qualitative Description of Search (Poor, Average, Great): **Narrative**_____

Estimate of Forward Speed of Search (Fast, Normal, Slow): _____

Was there any gaps in the area searched? YES NO *If YES, explain*: _____

Was the team adequately equipped?   YES NO *If NO, explain*: _____

Rate the team's composition? (Poor, Average, Great): **Narrative**: _____

Rate the team's performance? (Poor, Average, Great): **Narrative**: _____

Rate the team's morale?   (Poor, Average, Great): **Narrative**: _____

Is the team ready for another task? YES NO *If NO, explain*: _____

Did the team use a GPS? YES NO *If Yes, Did Debriefer download data?* _____

DOG TASKS:

Wind direction, speed and variability: _____

Direction and strength of alerts: _____

Was the scent article adequate? YES NO *If NO, explain*:_____

TEAM LEADER'S COMMENTS OR FOLLOW-UP RECOMMENDATIONS:
_____
_____

Searchers Observations: _____
_____

Recommendations for Re-search of Area: _____
_____

DEBRIEFER'S SECTION:

Required Follow-up:_____
_____

Comments: _____

Reviewed by Operations Section Chief: _____ Date / Time:_____

Routing Instructions: Initials   Follow-up action taken:_____

Plans/Investigations ❏   _____   _____

IC / Search Mgr.   ❏   _____   _____

_____ ❏   _____   _____

ATTACHED THE TEAMS MAP WITH THE DEBRIEFING SHEET. MARK ALERTS/CLUES AND TRACK ON MAP.

INCIDENT RADIO COMMUNICATIONS PLAN (ICS 205)

1. Incident Name:

2. Date/Time Prepared:
Date:
Time:

3. Operational Period:
Date From:
Time From:
Date To:
Time To:

4. Basic Radio Channel Use:

Zone Grp.	Ch #	Function	Channel Name/Trunked Radio System Talkgroup	Assignment	RX Freq N or W	RX Tone/NAC	TX Freq N or W	TX Tone/NAC	Mode (A, D, or M)	Remarks

5. Special Instructions:

6. Prepared by (Communications Unit Leader): Name: _____ Signature: _____

ICS 205 | IAP Page _____ | Date/Time: _____

COMMUNICATIONS LIST (ICS 205A)

1. Incident Name:	2. Operational Period: Date From:	Date To:
	Time From:	Time To:

3. Basic Local Communications Information:

Incident Assigned Position	Name (Alphabetized)	Method(s) of Contact (phone, pager, cell, etc.)

4. Prepared by: Name: _____ Position/Title: _____ Signature: _____

| ICS 205A | IAP Page _____ | Date/Time: _____ |

MEDICAL PLAN (ICS 206)

1. Incident Name:	2. Operational Period: Date From: / Date To: / Time From: / Time To:

3. Medical Aid Stations:

Name	Location	Contact Number(s)/Frequency	Paramedics on Site?
			☐ Yes ☐ No
			☐ Yes ☐ No
			☐ Yes ☐ No
			☐ Yes ☐ No
			☐ Yes ☐ No
			☐ Yes ☐ No

4. Transportation (indicate air or ground):

Ambulance Service	Location	Contact Number(s)/Frequency	Level of Service
			☐ ALS ☐ BLS
			☐ ALS ☐ BLS
			☐ ALS ☐ BLS
			☐ ALS ☐ BLS

5. Hospitals:

Hospital Name	Address, Latitude & Longitude if Helipad	Contact Number(s)/ Frequency	Travel Time Air	Travel Time Ground	Trauma Center	Burn Center	Helipad
					☐ Yes Level:____	☐ Yes ☐ No	☐ Yes ☐ No
					☐ Yes Level:____	☐ Yes ☐ No	☐ Yes ☐ No
					☐ Yes Level:____	☐ Yes ☐ No	☐ Yes ☐ No
					☐ Yes Level:____	☐ Yes ☐ No	☐ Yes ☐ No
					☐ Yes Level:____	☐ Yes ☐ No	☐ Yes ☐ No

6. Special Medical Emergency Procedures:

☐ Check box if aviation assets are utilized for rescue. If assets are used, coordinate with Air Operations.

7. Prepared by (Medical Unit Leader): Name: _____ Signature: _____

8. Approved by (Safety Officer): Name: _____ Signature: _____

| ICS 206 | IAP Page ____ | Date/Time: _____ |

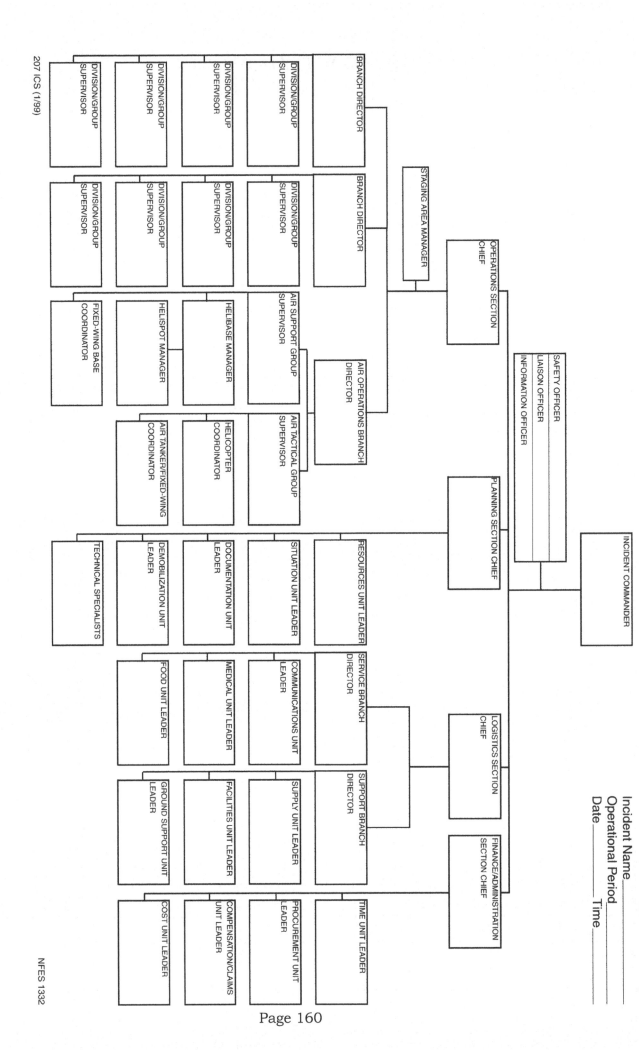

INCIDENT ORGANIZATION CHART (ICS 207)

| 1. Incident Name: | 2. Operational Period: | Date From: | Date To: |
| | | Time From: | Time To: |

3. Organization Chart

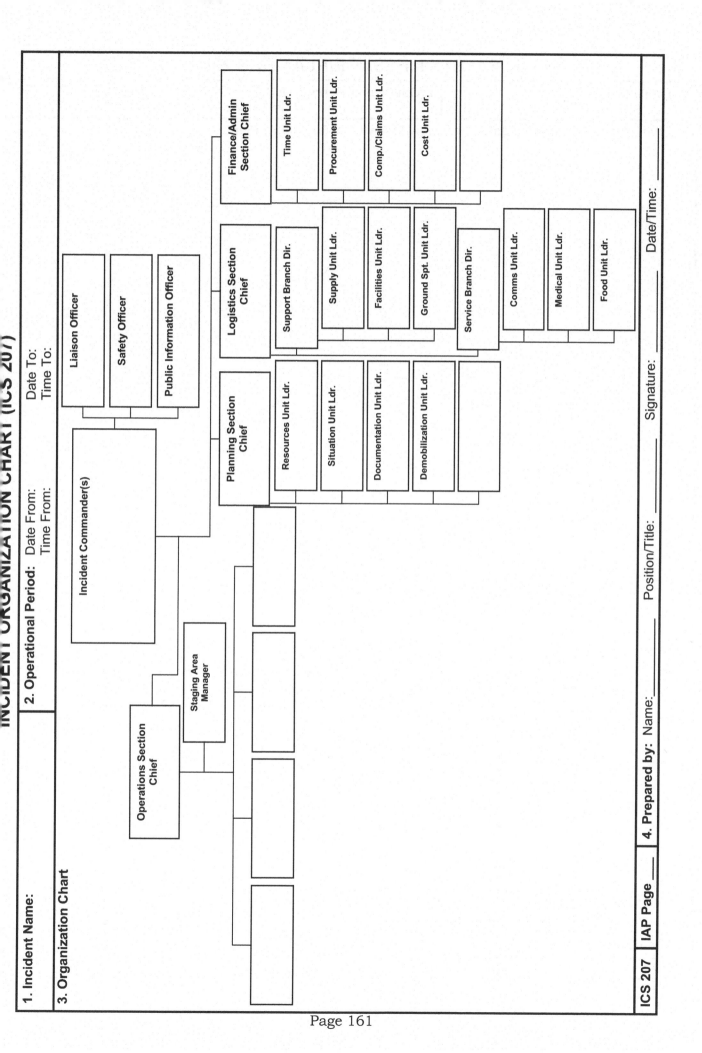

| ICS 207 | IAP Page ___ | 4. Prepared by: Name: ___ | Position/Title: ___ | Signature: ___ | Date/Time: ___ |

SAFETY MESSAGE/PLAN (ICS 208)

| 1. Incident Name: | 2. Operational Period: Date From: Date To: |
| | Time From: Time To: |

3. Safety Message/Expanded Safety Message, Safety Plan, Site Safety Plan:

4. Site Safety Plan Required? Yes ☐ No ☐
  Approved Site Safety Plan(s) Located At:

5. Prepared by: Name: _____ Position/Title: _____ Signature: _____

| ICS 208 | IAP Page _____ | Date/Time: _____ |

RESOURCE STATUS CHANGE (ICS 210)

| 1. Incident Name: | 2. Operational Period: | Date From: | Date To: |
| | | Time From: | Time To: |

3. Resource Number	4. New Status (Available, Assigned, O/S)	5. From (Assignment and Status):	6. To (Assignment and Status):	7. Time and Date of Change:	

8. Comments:

9. Prepared by: Name: _____ Position/Title: _____ Signature: _____

ICS 210   Date/Time: _____

CHECK-IN LIST

1. INCIDENT NAME

2. CHECK-IN LOCATION
☐ BASE ☐ CAMP ☐ STAGING AREA ☐ ICP RESOURCES ☐ HELIBASE

3. DATE/TIME

CHECK-IN INFORMATION

4. PERSONNEL (OVERHEAD) BY AGENCY & NAME -OR- LIST EQUIPMENT BY THE FOLLOWING FORMAT

AGENCY SINGLE T/F S/T	KIND	TYPE	I.D. NO./NAME	5. ORDER/ REQUEST NUMBER	6. DATE/TIME CHECK-IN	7. LEADER'S NAME	8. TOTAL NO. PERSONNEL	9. MANIFEST YES | NO	10. CREW WEIGHT INDIVIDUAL WEIGHT	11. HOME BASE	12. DEPARTURE POINT	13. METHOD OF TRAVEL	14. INCIDENT ASSIGNMENT	15. OTHER QUALIFICATION	16. SENT TO RESOURCES TIME/INT.

17. PAGE ____ OF ____

18. PREPARED BY (NAME AND POSITION)

USE BACK FOR REMARKS OR COMMENTS

211 ICS (1/99)

NFES 1335

ACTIVITY LOG (ICS 214)

| 1. Incident Name: | 2. Operational Period: | Date From: | Date To: |
| | | Time From: | Time To: |

3. Name:	4. ICS Position:	5. Home Agency (and Unit):

6. Resources Assigned:

Name	ICS Position	Home Agency (and Unit)

7. Activity Log:

Date/Time	Notable Activities

8. Prepared by: Name: _____ Position/Title: _____ Signature: _____

ICS 214, Page 1   Date/Time: _____

ACTIVITY LOG (ICS 214)

| 1. Incident Name: | 2. Operational Period: | Date From: | Date To: |
| | | Time From: | Time To: |

7. Activity Log (continuation):

Date/Time	Notable Activities

8. Prepared by: Name: _____ Position/Title: _____ Signature: _____

ICS 214, Page 2 Date/Time: _____

SEARCH AND RESCUE
SAR UNIT PERSONNEL REGISTER

| DATE | NAME OF INCIDENT | | LOCATION COUNTY | | POLICE CC # | | PAGE | OF |

NAME (LAST,FIRST,MI)	ORGANIZATION	TEAM ID Radio Call Sign	SAR QUALIFICATIONS	EMERGENCY CONTACT	ARRIVAL DATE/TIME	DEPARTURE DATE/TIME

ICS-211 (SAR)

DAILY CLUE LOG

INCIDENT: _____ DATE: _____ Page _____ of _____ Pages

CLUE #	TASK #	Time Found	Map Coord.	CLUE DESCRIPTION	ACTION TAKEN	IC INIT.

SEARCH BRIEFING

Date:_____ Time:_____ Operational Period: _____

Primary Agency: _____ CC#:_____ Initial Time:_____

Incident Commander: _____ Search Manager:_____

Operations: _____ Briefer/Debriefer:_____

Search Subject Information:

Name:_____

Age: _____ DOB:_____

Heights: _____ Weight: _____

Hair Color: _____ Eye Color:_____

Facial Hair:_____

Glasses/Contacts: _____

Other Distinguishing Marks: _____

Clothing Description: _____

Footwear: (Type and Size):_____

Equipment:_____

Vehicle Description:

    Make: _____ Model: _____ Color: _____

    Year:_____ Plate:_____ State: _____

PHOTO

Medical Condition: _____

Experience: _____

Situation Summary:

_____

_____

_____

Actions Taken So Far/ Resources on Scene:

_____

Communications Plan (Radio Frequency, Cell #'s)

_____

Medical Plan:_____

Weather Summary: _____

MISSING

NAME: _____ AGE: _____ DOB: _____

PHYSICAL DESCRIPTION:

SEX: _____ RACE: _____ HT: _____ WT: _____ BUILD: _____

HAIR COLOR: _____ LENGTH: _____ STYLE: _____

EYE COLOR: _____ GLASSES (Type/Style): _____ CONTACTS: _____

MEDICATIONS (for what): _____

DISTINGUISHING MARKS, SCARS: _____

MEDICAL PROBLEMS/DISABILITIES: _____

PHYSICAL CONDITION: _____

MENTAL CONDITION: _____

SMOKER/TOBACCO CHEWER: _____ OTHER HABITS: _____

CLOTHING/EQUIPMENT DESCRIPTION:

SHIRT: COLOR:_____ STYLE:_____
PANTS: COLOR:_____ STYLE:_____
FOOTGEAR:COLOR:_____ STYLE:_____
SOCKS: COLOR:_____ STYLE:_____
COAT: COLOR:_____ STYLE:_____
SWEATER: COLOR:_____ STYLE:_____
HAT: COLOR:_____ STYLE:_____
PACK: COLOR:_____ STYLE:_____
OTHER:_____
_____

EXPERIENCE:
FAMILIAR WITH AREA?_____ HOW RECENTLY:_____

GENERAL EXPERIENCE:_____

SITUATION:
PLS: _____ WHEN (Date/Time): _____

WHAT HAPPENED: _____
_____
_____

(ATTACH PHOTO)

INTERVIEWER:

Date:_____ Time:_____ Mission No:_____

Interviewer:_____ Title:_____ Agency:_____

Information given by:_____ Phone #:_____

LOST PERSON

NAME:_____
       (LAST)   (FIRST)   (MIDDLE)

NICKNAME(S)_____ ALIASES:_____

Occupation: _____

Local Address: _____

Home Address: (Street) _____

      (City):_____ (State)_____ (Zip):_____

Local Phone:_____ Home Phone: _____

PHYSICAL DESCRIPTION:

AGE:_____ SEX: _____ RACE:_____ HT:_____ WT:_____ BUILD:_____

HAIR COLOR:_____ LENGTH:_____ STYLE:_____

SIDEBURNS: _____ BEARD:_____ MUSTACHE:_____

BALDING? _____ Describe:_____

EYE COLOR:_____ GLASSES?:_____ REGULAR____ SUN____ CONTACTS:___

Facial features/shape: _____
Complexion:_____

TEETH (Normal, Gaps, Chipped, Decayed, Protruding) :_____ MEDICATIONS: _____

DISTINGUISHING MARKS, SCARS:_____

DISABILITIES:_____

GENERAL APPEARANCE:_____

PHYSICAL CONDITION:_____

MENTAL CONDITION:_____

CLOTHING WORN:

HAT: YES ☐ NO☐   STYLE:_____   COLOR:_____

SHIRT: YES ☐ NO ☐   STYLE:_____   COLOR:_____

SWEATER: YES ☐ NO ☐   STYLE:_____   COLOR:_____

JACKET: YES ☐ NO ☐   STYLE:_____   COLOR:_____

PANTS: YES ☐ NO ☐   STYLE:_____   COLOR:_____

RAINGEAR: YES ☐ NO ☐   STYLE:_____   COLOR:_____

FOOTGEAR: YES ☐ NO ☐   STYLE:_____   COLOR:_____

GLOVES: YES ☐ NO ☐   STYLE:_____   COLOR:_____

SOCKS: YES ☐ NO ☐   STYLE:_____   COLOR:_____

OTHER:_____   STYLE:_____   COLOR:_____

EQUIPMENT:

PACK (Brand/Style):_____   COLOR:_____

EXTRA CLOTHING:_____

FOOD & WATER: _____

SKIS, GUN, FISHING, CAMERA, ECT.:_____

OTHER EQUIPMENT CARRIED: KEYS:___ MONEY:____ KNIFE:____ FLASHLIGHT:___

_____

EXPERIENCE:

FAMILIAR WITH AREA?_____ HOW RECENTLY:_____

GENERAL EXPERIENCE:_____

OUTDOOR EXPERIENCE: SCOUTS ☐ MILITARY ☐ HUNTING ☐ BERRYPICKING☐
     BACKPACKING ☐ CLIMBING ☐ HIKING:Trails ☐ Cross Country ☐

EXPLAIN:_____

EVER BEEN LOST BEFORE: YES ☐ NO ☐ FOUND WHERE:_____

FROM THE LOCAL AREA: YES ☐ NO ☐

TRIP PLANS:

POINT LAST SEEN (BE SPECIFIC): _____

_____
IS THE POINT LAST SEEN MARKED AND SECUREDii

DATE/TIME LAST SEEN: Date:_____ DOW:_____ TIME:_____

LAST SEEN BY WHOM: _____ PHONE:_____

DESTINATION:_____

PROPOSED ROUTE:_____

REASON FOR LEAVING:_____

Date/time due and meeting
place:_____

ARE THERE OTHERS IN PARTY: YES ❏   NO ❏   HOW MANY:_____

SOURCE OF REPORT:

Person Reporting: Name: (Last): _____ (first:)_____ (mi:)____

Relationship to the missing
person:_____

Address (street, city, st, zip):_____

Home Phone:_____ Work Phone:_____

PICTURE OF MISSING PERSON:

HOW OLD IS PICTURE:_____

THIS __DOES NOT__ REPLACE FILLING OUT THE __STATE OF MARYLAND MISSING PERSONS REPORT!__

BRIEF DESCRIPTION OF SITUATION:_____
_____
_____
_____

VEHICLE DESCRIPTION: (Used by the Missing Subject)   **Vehicle Recovered:**_____

Year:_____ Make:_____ Model:_____ Colors:_____

Any Distinguishing Marks or Characteristics on or about the Vehicle:_____
_____

Vehicle Registered to Whom:_____ Tag Number/St.:_____

VIN #:_____ If Recovered, Where:_____

Time/Date of Vehicle found/recovered:_____ By Whom:_____

HABITS/PERSONALITY:

SMOKE:YES❑ NO❑ If so, Brand/how often/what:_____
    Does the person Bite the butts of the cirgarette YES❑ NO❑

ALCOHOL: YES❑ NO❑ If so, Brand/how often/what:_____

RECREATIONAL DRUG: YES❑ NO❑ If so what/how often:_____

GUM: YES❑ NO❑ If so, Brand/how often:_____

OUTGOING/QUIET/LONER/SOCIABLE:_____

DO THEY GIVE UP EASY OR KEEP GOING:_____

WHAT HOBBIES/INTERESTS:_____
_____

ANY CRIMINAL HISTORY OR LEGAL PROBLEMS: YES❑ NO❑ If Yes, What:_____
_____

PERSONAL PROBLEMS:_____
_____

ANY PERSONAL VALUES OR PHILOSOPHYS:_____
_____

Coverage to Probability of Detection (POD) Chart

Coverage	POD %	Coverage	POD %	Coverage	POD %	Coverage	POD %
0.100	10%	1.025	64%	2.025	87%	3.025	95%
0.125	12%	1.050	65%	2.050	87%	3.050	95%
0.150	14%	1.075	66%	2.075	87%	3.075	95%
0.175	16%	1.100	67%	2.100	88%	3.100	95%
0.200	18%	1.125	68%	2.125	88%	3.125	96%
0.225	20%	1.150	68%	2.150	88%	3.150	96%
0.250	22%	1.175	69%	2.175	89%	3.175	96%
0.275	24%	1.200	70%	2.200	89%	3.200	96%
0.300	26%	1.225	71%	2.225	89%	3.225	96%
0.325	28%	1.250	71%	2.250	89%	3.250	96%
0.350	30%	1.275	72%	2.275	90%	3.275	96%
0.375	31%	1.300	73%	2.300	90%	3.300	96%
0.400	33%	1.325	73%	2.325	90%	3.325	96%
0.425	35%	1.350	74%	2.350	90%	3.350	96%
0.450	36%	1.375	75%	2.375	91%	3.375	97%
0.475	38%	1.400	75%	2.400	91%	3.400	97%
0.500	39%	1.425	76%	2.425	91%	3.425	97%
0.525	41%	1.450	77%	2.450	91%	3.450	97%
0.550	42%	1.475	77%	2.475	92%	3.475	97%
0.575	44%	1.500	78%	2.500	92%	3.500	97%
0.600	45%	1.525	78%	2.525	92%	3.525	97%
0.625	46%	1.550	79%	2.550	92%	3.550	97%
0.650	48%	1.575	79%	2.575	92%	3.575	97%
0.675	49%	1.600	80%	2.600	93%	3.600	97%
0.700	50%	1.625	80%	2.625	93%	3.625	97%
0.725	52%	1.650	81%	2.650	93%	3.650	97%
0.750	53%	1.675	81%	2.675	93%	3.675	97%
0.775	54%	1.700	82%	2.700	93%	3.700	98%
0.800	55%	1.725	82%	2.725	93%	3.725	98%
0.825	56%	1.750	83%	2.750	94%	3.750	98%
0.850	57%	1.775	83%	2.775	94%	3.775	98%
0.875	58%	1.800	83%	2.800	94%	3.800	98%
0.900	59%	1.825	84%	2.825	94%	3.825	98%
0.925	60%	1.850	84%	2.850	94%	3.850	98%
0.950	61%	1.875	85%	2.875	94%	3.875	98%
0.975	62%	1.900	85%	2.900	94%	3.900	98%
1.000	63%	1.925	85%	2.925	95%	4.000	98%
		1.950	86%	2.950	95%		
		1.975	86%	2.975	95%		
		2.000	86%	3.000	95%		

$$POD = 1 - e^{-C}$$

Remember it is:
One minus the exponetial of
negative coverage.

c = Coverage
e = Exponetial

Coverage is the area covered
by the searcher divided by the
size of the search area

Created by: Cole Brown 2013   Page 175

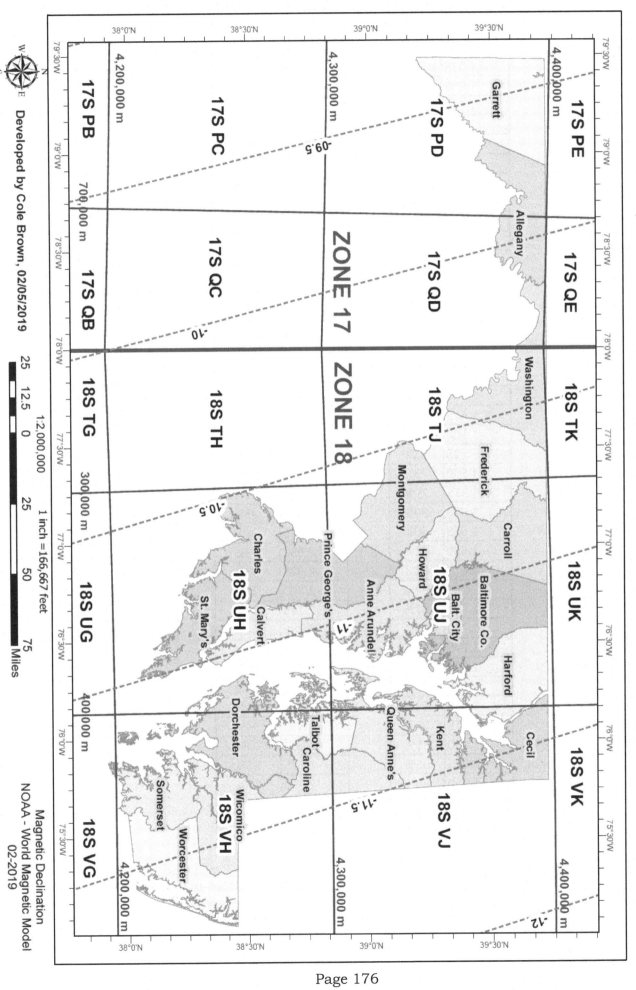

Maryland US National Grid
100,000 Meter Grid with GZD Zone Designator

Developed by Cole Brown, 02/05/2019

1:2,000,000

1 inch = 166,667 feet

Magnetic Declination
NOAA - World Magnetic Model
02-2019

Meter to Feet:

1 meter =	3.28 feet
10 meters =	32.80 feet
100 meters =	328.00 feet
1000 meters =	3,280.00 feet

1 Mile = 5,280 feet or 1,609.7 meters
1 Mile = 1.61 Kilometers

Latitude distance – based on an Arc and being a parallel distance
        1 Degree = 69 Miles or 364,320 feet
        1 Minute = 1.15 Miles or 6,072 feet
        1 Second = 101.2 feet

Longitude Distance at equator 1 degree is 69 miles, but at 39 degrees:
        1 degree is 54 miles or 285,120 feet
        1 Minute = 0.9 miles or 4,752 feet
        1 Second = 79.2 feet

Circle = 360 degrees   1 degree = 60 minutes   1 minutes = 60 seconds

Acres:
        1 Acre has 43,560 sq. ft. – 208.71 ft. x 208.71 ft. = 43,560 sq. ft.
        1 Acre has 4,047 sq. m. – 63.62 m x 63.62 m = 4,047 sq. m.

	Meters	Meters	Sq. Meters	Acres per	Rounded
1 square on Grid Reader	100	100	10,000	2.468	2.5 Acres
25 squares on Grid Reader	500	500	250,000	61.698	62 Acres
100 squares on Grid Reader	1000	1000	1,000,000	246.792	250 Acres

Figuring acreage using the grid reader.

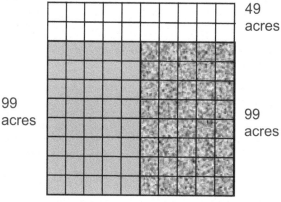

49 acres

99 acres

99 acres

100 Acres = 404,686 square meters or 404.686 square Kilometers

1 square Kilometer has 250 acres on flat ground and will take 3 airscent dogs to cover the area in 3.5 hours. 85 acres per dog. Three Ground Teams can also cover the same area.

TIME

328 ft or 100 meters takes an average person 1 minute and 15 seconds to walk.
It takes a person to cover an acre of area approximately 2 minutes.

With this information we can calculate the approximate time to search 100 acres of area which is 3.5 hours or 210 minutes.

Each 100 meter square block equaling 2.468 acres takes approximately 5 minutes to cover.

Applying Search Resources
Tactical Deployment

There are two basic modes involved in Search Tactics:
- *Passive*
- *Active*

Passive Techniques
- Wait
- Confinement and Containment
- Attraction
- Investigation

Confinement and Containment Mode
- Tagged String Lines
- Road Blocks
- Tail Blocks
- Track Traps
- Camp ins
- Lookouts
- Radio Relays

Attraction Mode:
- Visual Attraction
- Sound Attraction
- Media
- Aircraft Fly-over

Applying Search Resources
Tactical Deployment

Active Techniques
Type I - *Speed*
Type II - *Efficiency*
Type III - *Thoroughness*

Type I Techniques
- Investigation
- Hasty Teams - 3 person teams
- Thorough checks of Last Know Location
- Following Known Routes
- Trail Running
- Perimeter Check
- Sign Cutting/ Man-Tracking
- Road Patrols
- Check Attractions
- Check Hazardous Areas
- Check Drainage's
- Ridge Running
- Bastard Search
- Locating any Clues
- ELT/PLB/Direction Finding Search
- Airscent Dog along the perimeter, road, trail, or drainage
- Bloodhound or trailing dog from Point Last Seen or Last Know Point

Type II Techniques
- 6 person Hasty teams searching in defined search area.
  - ✓ Open Grid Search
  - ✓ Sound Sweep
  - ✓ Critical Separation
    - Purposeful Wandering
    - 360 degree turn techniques
  - ✓ Along a Ravine, Road, or Creek (Parallel Search)
- Airscent Dog assigned to a segment
- Helicopter search using FLIR or Day Camera (Record if possible)

Type III Techniques
- Large ground search teams with closed spacing search a defined area.

Reflex Tasking Worksheet

Wheel Elements	Steps	Tasks
Axle	① Plot the IPP.	✓ Preserve IPP ✓ Immediate locale search ✓ If a structure, search and re-search repeatedly ✓ Signcutters/trackers ✓ Tracking/trailing dogs
Rim	② Determine subject category. ③ Determine statistical ring. ④ Draw 50% and 95% rings. ⑤ Reduce search area using subjective and deductive reasoning. ⑥ Mark boundary on map.	✓ Establish containment. ✓ Consider camp-ins, road/trail blocks, track traps, patrols, attraction, and string lines.
Hub	⑦ Mark 25% ring if appropriate.	✓ Canvass campgrounds, if appropriate. ✓ Thoroughly search from IPP to 25% when less than 0.2 miles/0.3 km.
Spokes	⑧ Draw travel routes: • Blue lines (water features, drainages) • Dashed lines (trails) • Black/red lines (roads, man-made features) • Travel corridors (ridges, contours) • Corridor tasks, if appropriate	✓ Conduct hasty search of trails, roads, drainages, and other travel routes leading away from IPP. **Emphasis at likely decision points.**
Reflector	⑨ Mark high probability/hazard areas.	✓ Send hasty teams to areas of high probability, high hazard, historic locations of finds.
	⑩ Prioritize and deploy tasks using quick consensus method.	

Search Theory Definitions and Coverage vs. POD

Area Effectively Swept (Z) - A measure of the area that can be (or was) effectively searched by searchers within the limits of search speed, endurance, and effective sweep width. The area effectively swept (Z) equals the effective sweep width (W) times search speed (V) times hours spent in the search area (T). That is, $Z = (W \times V) \times T$ for one searcher or one resource (such as a ground searcher, dog team, boat, or aircraft and its crew).

Coverage (C) - The ratio of the area effectively swept (Z) to the area searched (A), that is, $C = Z/A$. Coverage may be thought of as a measure of "thoroughness." The probability of detection (POD) of a search is determined by the coverage

Effective Sweep Width (W) - A measure of the effectiveness with which a particular sensor can detect a particular object under specific environmental conditions; a measure of detectability. Effective sweep width depends on the search object, the sensor, and the environmental conditions prevailing at the time and place of the search. There is no simple or intuitive definition, although it is possible to illustrate the concept.

Effort (z or TLL) - a.k.a., **Track Line Length**. The total distance traveled by all searchers (or a boat or aircraft and its crew) while searching in the assigned segment. Loosely speaking, the number of searcher-hours expended while searching can be called "effort," but without knowing the average search speed, it cannot be used to compute coverage.

Probability of Area (POA) - (also, Probability of Containment [POC]). The probability that the search object is contained within the boundaries of a region, segment, or other geographic area.

Probability of Detection (POD) - The probability of the search object being detected, assuming it was in the segment searched. POD measures sensor effectiveness, thoroughness, and quality. POD is a function of the coverage (C) achieved in the segment (see Figure 14-4).

Probability of Success (POS) - The probability of finding the search object with a particular search. pas measures search effectiveness. The accumulated probability of finding the search object with all the search effort expended over all searches to date is called "cumulative pas" (POScum).

Region - A subset of the search area based only on factors that affect POA; that is, regions may require segmentation prior to searching. Regions are based on probability of the search object's location, not on suitability for assigning search resources. A region may contain searchable segments, or a region itself may be a searchable segment. A searchable segment may also contain one or more regions (based on probability), but rarely are the available data good enough to distinguish such small regions in ground search situations.

Search Area - The area determined by the search planner where SAR personnel will look for a search object. The search area includes the smallest area, consistent with all available information, which contains all of the possible search object locations, and therefore includes all regions and segments. The search area may be divided into regions based on the probable scenarios and into segments for the purpose of assigning specific tasks to the available search resources.

Search Object - A ship, aircraft, or other craft missing or in distress, or survivors, or related search objects, persons, or evidence for which a search is being conducted. A generic term used to indicate the lost person or evidence (clue) related to a lost subject. In the same segment, different search objects generally have different effective sweep widths (or "detectabilities"). This means that for any given search of a segment, different coverage areas, and hence different POD values, will be achieved for different search objects. A live, human search object is often referred to as a search subject.

Search Speed (V) - The average rate of travel (speed over the ground) of searchers while engaged in search operations within a segment.

Segment - A designated subarea (subset of the search area) to be searched by one or more specifically assigned search resources. The search planner determines the size of a segment. The boundaries of a segment are identifiable both in the field and on a map, and are based on suitability for assigning search resources, not probability of the search object's location.

Sensor - Human senses (sight, hearing, touch, etc.), those of specially trained animals (such as dogs), or electronic devices used to detect the object of a search. A human, multi-sensor platform is often referred to as a "searcher."

Definitions from NASAR Fundamental of Search and Rescue copyrighted 2005

Search Theory Definitions and Coverage vs. POD

Figure 14-4 NASAR – Fundamental of Search and Rescue

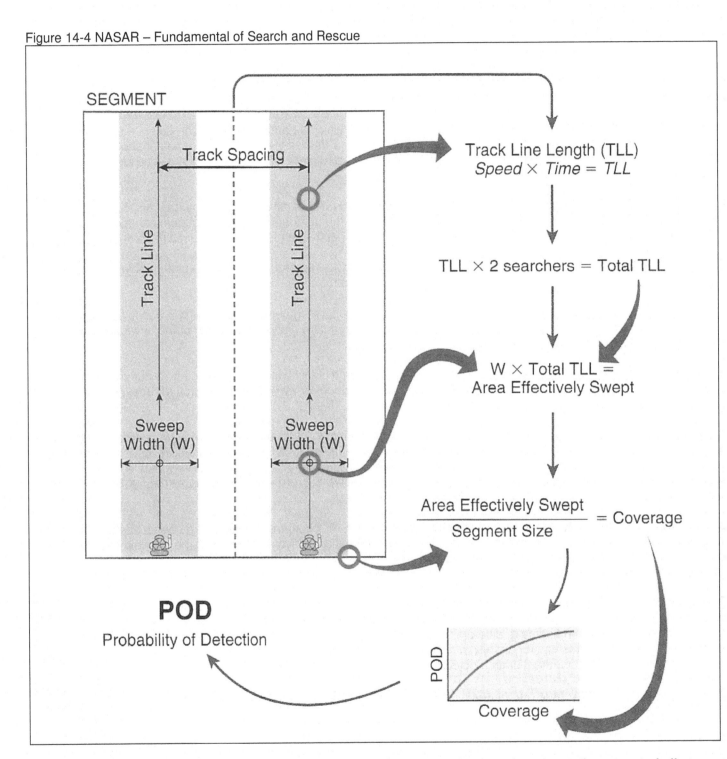

Figure 14-4: Detection elements of search theory. As searchers pass though a search segment, the amount of effort expended in the segment increases. Probability of Detection is computed by multiplying the sweep width (W) by the Track Line Length (TLL; a measure of effort) and dividing the result, called the "area effectively swept," by the area of the segment. The final number is the "coverage" from which POD can be determined by using a "POD versus coverage" chart. In the graph, the area effectively swept (orange area) equals one-half the size of the segment, so the coverage is 0.5. The POD for a coverage of 0.5 is 39%.

Search Theory Definitions and Coverage vs. POD

% POD vs. Coverage

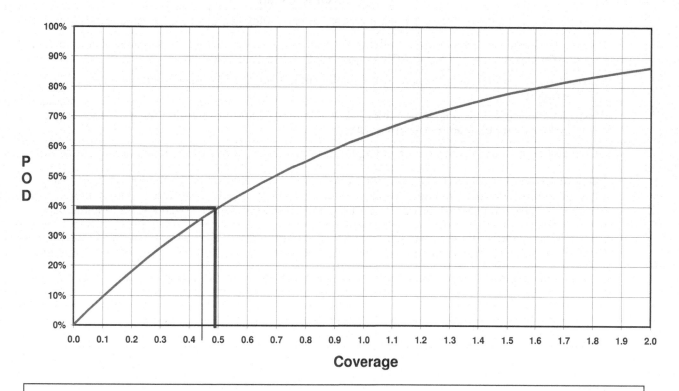

Coverage

Information to report to Search Managers (Planners) after a Search:

Several important pieces of information that affect search planning should be conveyed to search planners by field personnel after an area or linear search is conducted:

1. Estimated forward search speed of the individual or team while searching.
2. How long the individual or team searched (excluding rest breaks and such)
3. Field measurement of average maximum detection range (AMDR) or some similar field observable measure. [Sweep Width (W)]
4. Other field-observable measures identified and requested by search planners prior to assignment.
5. A qualitative description of how well the team did with the search (e.g. excellent, good, fair, or poor)
6. A qualitative description of the search conditions (e.g. rough terrain that slowed and fatigued searchers, numerous thickets that could not be thoroughly investigated and still finish the assignment on time, etc.) Where there any gaps in the search area.

Forward Search Speed
Normal speed can be 4 to 5 minutes for every 100 meters.

Slow =   0.5 x Normal Speed
Normal =   1.0 x Normal Speed
Fast =   1.5 x Normal Speed

If search planners know how fast searchers are traveling (v) and exactly how long they have been searching (t) the Track Line Length can be calculated (TLL) V x t = TLL.

First Arriving Law Enforcement Officer
Checklist for Search of a Missing Person

Completed	Action Taken
	Conduct a rapid assessment of situation and a complete interview of all witnesses and complainants
	Develop a basic synopsis of the situation and basic physical and clothing description of the missing person for Duty Officer (DO) and PCO to give "BOLO" [**Be On Look Out**].
	Determine in the case of a missing child if the incident is an abduction and warrants a request for an "Amber Alert"
	Establish on scene Incident Commander (IC) and initiate Incident Command System according to National Incident Management System (NIMS).
	Begin MPR and initiate a log documenting the date and times of all actions taken during the search
	Determine and secure the Point Last Seen (PLS) or the Last Known Position (LKP) of the missing person and prevent or eliminate anything from destroying the scent. Examples would be exhaust from motor vehicles and establishing command post and vehicle/personnel staging at immediate scene.
	Search the interior of the entire residence or building where the person was last seen. (Close attention should be paid to underneath beds, closets, etc.) Repeat this every 30 minute by different personnel.
	Begin roving patrols of the area on all roadways leading away from PLS and/or LKP.
	Establish a perimeter at a minimum of ½ mile from Point Last Seen (PLS) or Last Known Position (LKP). With vehicles or personnel at main roadways leading away from Point Last Seen.
	Search all outbuildings on the property of the missing subject (be careful not to contaminant area)
	Conduct an assessment of the situation and complete a search urgency evaluation.
	Request specialized and qualified resources to respond to the scene: Law Enforcement Special Operations and Aviation Command: • A bloodhound • A search manager • A helicopter • A command vehicle
	Prepare areas for aviation to search and when aviation arrives, brief and direct aviation division for an aerial search of the area. Obtain Latitude and Longitude Coordinates of PLS/LKP.
	Determine areas close by that can be used for a command post and staging area for incoming resources. (Consider area where helicopter could land and to stage and be briefed **face to face**)
	Secure all scent articles that have been previously touched by the victim using the following procedures: • Always use rubber gloves. • Keep articles separate and do not allow them to touch each other which may cause cross contamination • Place separated articles inside of clear plastic or evidence bags (do not use a standard trash bag because of the deodorizers that are used in them which can mask the scent for the canine)
	Begin a neighborhood check of the entire area – begin with immediate neighbors. Consider using reverse 911 or a "Child is Missing" Services - (888) 875-2246.
	Contact all friends and family to determine the victim's location
	Check all areas that victim frequents (malls, schools, work, restaurants, lounges, etc.)
	Check area hospitals, emergency services, shelters, and taxi and bus services
	Determine if any vehicles are missing in the area, if the victim drives
	Contact the assistance of a criminal investigator, if warranted, to assist with any electronic tracking of cell phones, bank accounts, credit card statements, etc.
	Repeat the search of interior of the entire residence or building where the person was last seen by different law enforcement personnel. (Close attention should be paid to underneath beds, closets, etc.)

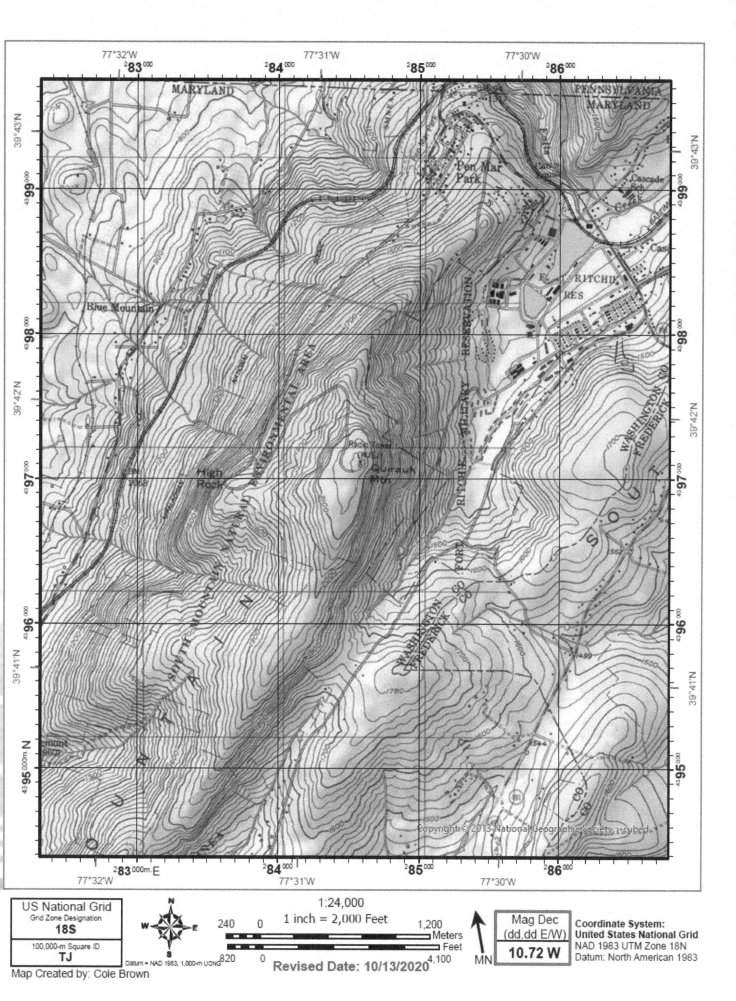

US National Grid
Grid Zone Designation
18S

100,000-m Square ID
TJ

Map Created by: Cole Brown

Datum = NAD 1983, 1,000-m USNG

1:24,000
1 inch = 2,000 Feet

240   0   1,200
Meters
Feet
820   0   4,100
Revised Date: 10/13/2020

Mag Dec
(dd.dd E/W)
10.72 W

Coordinate System:
United States National Grid
NAD 1983 UTM Zone 18N
Datum: North American 1983